CELTIC
SAINTS
OF
IRELAND

CELTIC
SAINTS
OF
IRELAND

ELIZABETH REES

The
History
Press

Front cover illustration: Crucifixion at the centre of Muiredach's cross, Monasterboice, Louth. (Author's collection)
Back cover illustration: St Mary's Cathedral and round tower, Scattery Island, Clare. (Author's collection)

First published 2013

The History Press
The Mill, Brimscombe Port
Stroud, Gloucestershire, GL5 2QG
www.thehistorypress.co.uk

British Library Cataloguing in Publication Data.
A catalogue record for this book is available from the British Library.

ISBN 978 0 7524 7740 4

Typesetting and origination by The History Press
Printed in Great Britain

CONTENTS

PREFACE

This book is written as an introduction to the Celtic saints of Ireland. With a very few exceptions, the monks who wrote the *vitae*, or biographies, of the Celtic saints lived many centuries later. It is therefore impossible to reconstruct the lives of these early monks and nuns, and so we can no longer view them except through medieval eyes. However, archaeology, the study of site, of place names, inscribed stones and early texts offer us clues about how these men and women lived.

As a student I was inspired by Derwas Chitty, who introduced me to the Desert Fathers, and I was held spellbound by the lectures of E.G. Bowen, whose infectious enthusiasm for landscape archaeology and the Celtic saints encouraged generations of scholars to develop and refine his ideas. This led me on a quest to visit the sites where devotion to our early Christian forebears is imprinted on the ground.

I am not primarily a scholar: after leaving Oxford University I entered monastic life, and my approach to the Celtic saints is therefore that of a vowed celibate woman, who has chanted the psalms daily. I have sat in a dark church in the early mornings, listening to hunks of scripture, allowing them to gradually reframe me, for such is the general aim. I know the joys and challenges of living in community alongside other vowed women, and this leads me to ask questions and explore possible answers from within a living tradition.

I read Latin but not Irish: for this I depend on colleagues who advise me. I am fortunate to know Jonathan Wooding, Karen Jankulak and Thomas O'Loughlin, and to have met with other scholars along the way. It is quite possible that your favourite saint does not appear in this book, because there are a vast number of early Irish saints. Those wishing to research their local saint are advised to consult Professor Pádraig Ó Riain's *Dictionary of Irish Saints* (Four Courts Press, 2011). Within its 660 pages, almost all the known facts concerning over 1000 saints are accurately documented.

I am grateful to Dr Jonathan Wooding of the Centre for the Study of Religion in Celtic Societies at the University of Wales, Lampeter, for his helpful suggestions. Any errors are my own. I thank Thomas O'Loughlin, Professor of Historical Theology at Nottingham University, for permission to quote from his book, *Saint Patrick: the man and his works*. Thank you also to my sister, Frances Jones, for her two photos of *The Seven Churches* on the Aran Islands, and for scanning all the remaining photographs, which I took on my travels. My final thank you is to the saints who have enticed me to meet them 'at home' in the beautiful locations where they chose to live.

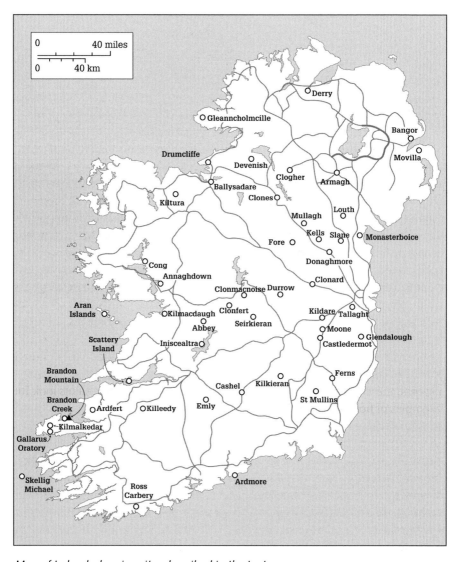

Map of Ireland, showing sites described in the text.

1

SAINTS IN THE DESERT

Sainthood

Most of the men and women whom we call the Celtic saints were monks and nuns. What did they think about sainthood? Their viewpoint was different from ours, because most of Church history had not yet happened. There were only four or five centuries of Christian men and women who could serve as models for holy living, and the more heroic among them had been martyred. While early monks and nuns may have read the Acts of the Martyrs, these accounts focussed on a martyr's death, rather than their life; they could not really be imitated.

Again, there were few models to imitate in the gospels: the first followers of Jesus are briefly described, but they are portrayed as disciples, rather than as people in their own right. We learn little about their personal holiness. The scriptures were written before monasteries existed, so where could models of holiness in a monastic context be found? St Paul does describe a Church in which virgins and widows have an accepted place; he does not, however, describe these women as people. To whom, then, did the Celtic saints look for examples of holy living?

Old Testament models

Celtic monks and nuns were deeply influenced by the Old Testament, since they were closer to it in time than we are. They were also, perhaps, better able to understand the mentalities and cultures of those who compiled the books within it. As Christians, of course, the gospels formed the foundation of their spiritual lives, and particular texts were held dear. Jesus had said 'If you wish to be perfect, go and sell what you own and give the money to the poor, ... then come, follow me' (Mt. 19. 21),[1] and this is what monks and nuns tried to do.

They often lived in groups; they came together and listened to the word of God, in order to 'be perfect', 'come' and 'follow'.

There was a model for this in the Old Testament: the First and Second Book of Kings describe brotherhoods of prophets who lived in the desert in quite large groups. Sometimes it is a group of fifty (2 Kgs. 2. 7; 17), under the leadership of someone wise and experienced, in this case Elijah, and his disciple Elisha, in the ninth century BC. Celtic monks could identify with a community who lived apart from society, under the authority of a holy person. As they listened to passages from scripture, read to them in church, day after day, they could connect with their Jewish-Christian heritage.

They knew that Jesus had pondered on the ministry of Elijah and Elisha, and had copied them too. Like Elisha, Jesus healed lepers, and he raised a widow's son to life, as both prophets had done. Luke portrays Jesus challenging the people of Nazareth by likening himself to his two great predecessors:

> There were many widows in Israel, I can assure you, in Elijah's day, when heaven remained shut for three years and six months and a great famine raged throughout the land, but Elijah was not sent to any of these: he was sent to a widow at Zarephath, a Sidonian town. And in the prophet Elisha's time there were many lepers in Israel, but none of these was cured, except the Syrian, Naaman (Lk. 4. 25-7).

When Jesus asked his disciples who people thought he might be, they replied: 'some say John the Baptist, some Elijah … or one of the prophets' (Mt. 16. 14).

Call to discipleship

Celtic monks would have resonated with the touching description of Elisha's unexpected call to leave his family in order to serve God. They would have understood his initial hesitation, followed by his generous response. As Elijah passed by, wearing his 'cloak of hair' and 'leather loincloth' (2 Kgs. 1. 8), he threw his cloak over Elisha, to claim him for God. Elisha appears to have been the model for the 'rich young man' of Matthew 19. 21: as a wealthy farmer, he owned twelve yoke of oxen. Yet unlike the rich man in Matthew's gospel who 'went away sad, for he was a man of great wealth', Elisha responded to Elijah's invitation. Like each Celtic monk, he underwent conversion, and exchanged his yoke of oxen for a life of discipleship under the yoke of a holy man:

> … [Elijah] came to Elisha son of Shaphat as he was ploughing behind twelve yoke of oxen, he himself being with the twelfth. Elijah passed near to him and threw his cloak over him. Elisha left his oxen and ran after Elijah. 'Let me kiss my father and mother, then I will follow you,' he said. Elijah answered,

'Go, go back; for have I done anything to you?' Elisha turned away, took the pair of oxen and slaughtered them. He used the plough for cooking the oxen, then gave to his men, who ate. He then rose, and followed Elijah and became his servant (1 Kgs. 19. 19-21).

The prophets model holiness

The so-called Elijah Cycle (1 Kgs. 17. 1 – 2 Kgs. 1. 18) and Elisha Cycle (2 Kgs. 2. 1 – 13. 21) recall the *vitae*, or Lives of Celtic saints: they were composed long after the deaths of their subjects, but they attempt to convey their core values and their holiness, for the edification of later generations of believers. We read of the miracles of Elijah and Elisha, which are often a compassionate response to the needs of a poor person or a local king. As in the *vitae*, the prophets are caught up in a world of intrigue and politics, and fearlessly challenge those in authority. Disciples are sent on errands by Elisha (2 Kgs. 9. 1-10), who himself learnt discipleship by washing the hands of Elijah (2 Kgs. 3. 11). The brotherhood makes simple mistakes: one of them unintentionally poisons the soup he has prepared, but Elisha makes it wholesome through his prayer (2 Kgs. 4. 38-41).

The Near Eastern Desert Fathers of the fourth century in some ways modelled their lives on these early prophets, and this may have been the reason that we find echoes of the prophets in the *vitae* of Celtic saints. In his *Life of Antony*, Athanasius records how 'Antony said to himself: "It is by looking at what the great Elijah does, as in a mirror, that the ascetic can always know what his own life should be like".'[2] The story of Antony's friend, Paul the Hermit, fed by a bird, reminds us of Elijah, whom God protects during a lengthy drought:

The word of the Lord came to [Elijah]: 'Go away from here, go eastward and hide yourself in the wadi Cherith which lies east of Jordan. You can drink from the stream, and I have ordered the ravens to bring you food there.' He did as the Lord had said; ... The ravens brought him bread in the morning and meat in the evening, and he quenched his thirst at the stream (1 Kgs. 17. 2-6).

In the same way, according to Jerome's *Life of Paul*, based on a Greek original, a raven brought half a loaf of bread each day to feed the hungry hermit.

Life in the desert

Elijah and Elisha were not the only Old Testament figures who offered inspiration to early Christians; if anything, life in the desert is a more constant theme. Discouraged by failure, Elijah journeys south through the desert, and climbs Mount Sinai. He hides in the cleft of the rock where Moses had crouched before him, and there God once again reveals his glory (1 Kgs. 19. 9; Ex. 33. 22). At the end of the Old Testament, the First Book of Maccabees, written in the second century BC, describes how the persecuted believers go and live in the desert:

> Mattathias went through the town, shouting at the top of his voice, 'Let everyone who has a fervour for the Law and takes his stand on the covenant come out and follow me.' Then he fled with his sons to the hills, leaving all their possessions behind in the town. At this, many who were concerned for virtue and justice went down to the desert and stayed there (1 Mac. 2. 27-9).

While these various Old Testament figures may have provided role models for Celtic monks, they offer us few clues about what went on in the heads and hearts of Celtic holy men and women. What were their values, and what governed their behaviour? How did they learn holiness? How did they become saints? In order to address these questions, we shall now look more closely at the traditions of the Desert Mothers and Fathers, who 'went down to the desert and stayed there' from the mid-third century AD onwards.

The Saying of the Desert Fathers

The Desert Mothers and Fathers were saints who immediately preceded those of Celtic times, and profoundly influenced them. The *Apothegmata*, or *Sayings of the Desert Fathers*, are brief anecdotes which were handed down as useful guidelines and cherished memories of the holy men and women who lived in the Near Eastern deserts. Collections of their Sayings were popular throughout medieval times, and they offer a unique range of personal beliefs and testimonies. They were treasured as advice on how to acquire holiness, and because of their brevity they could be memorised and pondered.

Stability
A number of the Sayings address the issue of stability, which has concerned monks down the ages. First, each monk built his hut. This was the place where he would discover himself and discover God: 'A brother came to Scetis to visit Abba Moses and asked him for a good word. The old man said to him: "Go, sit

in your cell, and your cell will teach you everything".[3] It was not a good idea to move from place to place. 'An old man said: "Just as a tree cannot bring forth fruit if it is always being transplanted, so the monk who is always going from one place to another is not able to bring forth virtue".[4] If you stayed away from your cell, you would die, like a fish on dry land. Athanasius records that Antony said: 'When fishes are out of water for some time, they die. So it is if monks stay a long time … out of their monastery'.[5]

Learning from others

However, you had to learn more about your new lifestyle somehow. You had to go and ask advice from those older and wiser than you. Dorotheus of Gaza said: 'To stay in one's hut is one half; and to go and see the old men is the other half'. It was a good idea to start off living as a disciple of one of them, so you could get a good grounding which would last a lifetime: 'Abba Isaiah said … to those who were making a good beginning by putting themselves under the direction of the holy Fathers: "As with purple dye, the first colouring is never lost".[6]

Later, you might live on your own, but even then, if you began to lose your sense of direction and became hardened, it was a good idea to go and join a wiser person than you: 'A brother asked Abba Paesios, "What should I do about my soul, because it is insensitive and does not fear God?" He replied, "Go and join a man who fears God, and live near him. He will teach you also to fear God".'

But in general you should work out your own spiritual way, ascetic or less so, according to your temperament. 'Abba Mark once said to Abba Arsenius, "It is good, is it not, to have nothing in your hut that gives you pleasure? For example, I once knew a brother who had a little wild flower that came up in his hut and he pulled it out by the roots". "Well," said Abba Arsenius, "That is all right. But each man should act according to his own spiritual way. And if one were not able to get along without the flower, he should plant it again".'[7]

Trusting one's judgment

It was foolish to let an unwise person be your guide: 'A brother questioned Abba Poeman, saying, "I am losing my soul through living near my abba; should I go on living with him?" The old man knew that he was finding this harmful, and he was surprised that he even asked if he should stay there. So he said to him, "Stay if you want to." The brother left him, and stayed on there. He came back again and said, "I am losing my soul." But the old man still did not tell him to leave. He came back a third time and said, "I really cannot stay there any longer." Then Abba Poeman said, "Now you are saving yourself; go away and do not stay with him any longer," and he added, "When someone sees that he is in danger of losing his soul, he does not need to ask advice".'[8]

Be silent and unknown

You could best find peace if you remained silent and unknown: 'Once a judge of the province came to see Abba Simon. The old man took off his leather girdle, and climbed a palm tree and began to prune it. When the people came up to him they said, "Where is the old man who lives in solitude here?" Abba Simon answered, "There is no solitary here". The judge went away.'[9]

It was better to be silent than to discuss even spiritual matters: 'Three Fathers used to go and visit blessed Antony every year, and two of them used to discuss their thoughts and the salvation of their souls with him, but the third always remained silent, and did not ask him anything. After a long time, Abba Antony said to him, "You often come here to see me but you never ask me anything," and the other replied, "It is enough for me to see you, Father".'[10]

Prayer

In your silence, prayer could flourish. Prayer would teach you everything: 'One of the elders said, "Pray attentively, and you will soon straighten out your thoughts".' Manual work helped one to pray: 'Someone asked a monk: "What must we do to be saved?" He was busy weaving baskets. Without even raising his eyes, he replied: "Do as you see".'[11]

By making ropes to be sold for the poor, one could cleave to God: 'A camel driver came one day to collect a bundle of ropes from Abba John the Dwarf. The monk went into his hut to fetch them, and forgot about him, his mind being set on God. The camel driver then knocked on his door. Again John came out, went in, and forgot. The camel driver knocked a third time, and again John came out. He went in again repeating "ropes, camel, ropes, camel", and so he managed to remember.'[12]

Another saying highlights the value of prayer: 'An old man came to see one of the Fathers, who cooked a few lentils and said to him, "Let us say a few prayers," and the first completed the whole psalter, and the brother recited the two great prophets by heart. When morning came, the visitor went away and they forgot the food'.[13] However, no one should be forced to pray: 'Some old men came to see Abba Poemen and said to him, "When we see the brothers who are dozing at the Prayers, should we wake them up so they will be more watchful?" He replied, "Well, when I see a brother who is dozing, I put his head on my knees, so he can rest".'[14]

Kindness

Charity was more important than an austere life. 'A brother came to visit Abba Macarius. After prayer he said: "Father, it is now forty years since I stopped eating meat, and I am still tempted by it". Macarius replied: "Don't say that to me but, I pray you, tell me: how many days have you spent without slandering your brother, without judging your neighbour?" The brother bowed his head and said, "Pray for me, Father, so that I may begin".'[15]

We should all think first of one another's needs: 'A brother brought a bunch of grapes to Abba Macarius, but he took it to another brother, who seemed more sick. The sick man thanked God for his brother's kindness, but took it to someone else, and he did the same. So the bunch of grapes was passed all around the cells, scattered over the desert, until at last it reached Abba Macarius again.'[16]

Such generosity was not achieved without a struggle, and it was never achieved completely. 'Abba Abraham said: "The passions live. In the saints they are only to some extent bound".'[17] A brother who was disturbed in mind went to Abba Theodore of Pherme and told him that he was troubled. Abba Theodore said, "Tell me now, how many years have you worn that habit?" The brother answered, "Eight". The old man replied, "Believe me, I have worn the habit seventy years, and have not yet found peace for a single day. Would you have peace in eight?"'[18]

Attitudes to women

The presence of groups of holy women living in the desert could pose problems for celibate men. Some of the *Sayings* reflect this: 'A nun was travelling with other sisters when she met a monk. When he caught sight of her, he made a detour. The nun told him: "If you were a true monk, you would not have even noticed that we were women".'[19]

Cassian relates how a monk could not bear to see the face, or even the clothes of a woman. One day he met a woman on his way, and fled to his monastery 'with as much speed and haste as if he had met a lion or a dragon'. Later, this monk became totally disabled. Not knowing how to nurse him themselves, the monks took him to a convent of nuns, where the nuns devoted themselves to his care for four years, until he died in their arms.[20]

At peace with animals

Athanasius wrote of Antony: 'It was an astonishing fact that alone in the desert, in the presence of so many wild beasts, he was not afraid of their ferocious nature; wild beasts lived at peace with him'. He describes how the animals obeyed Antony: 'The desert animals came to drink nearby, and they damaged Antony's young plants and seeds. But he gently took hold of one of the animals and told them all: "Why do you harm to me? I have done nothing to you. Go, and in the Lord's name, do not come back here again". And after that they kept away, as if they had heard what Antony said to them'.[21]

In other stories, lions wait on the monks, helping them fetch water and leading the donkey to pasture. Abba Agathon went to live in a cave in the desert, which already sheltered a large serpent. The snake, politely, wanted to leave, to give the monk some space, but Agathon was not to be outdone in politeness. He said: 'If you go, I won't settle here'. So the serpent stayed, and they both fed off a nearby sycamore tree.[22]

Love

In the end, love was all that mattered: 'Abba Pambo said, "If you have a heart, you can be saved".'[23] Love knows no half measures: those who give everything to God become irradiated by grace. 'Abba Lot went to see Abba Joseph and said to him, "Abba, as far as I can, I say my little office, I fast a little, I pray and meditate, I live in peace and as far as I can, I purify my thoughts. What else can I do?" Then the old man stood up and stretched his hands towards heaven. His fingers became like ten lamps of fire, and he said: "If you will, you can become all flame".'[24]

Nevertheless, greater love might be shown by leaving one's prayers and welcoming a visitor: 'A brother went to see an anchorite, and as he was leaving said to him, "Forgive me, abba, for having taken you away from your rule." But the other answered him, "My rule is to refresh you and send you away in peace".'[25]

Monastic pilgrims

Hermits offered peace and refreshment not only to brother monks but also to strangers and pilgrims. Some European monks and nuns visited the Near-Eastern deserts: to undertake such a pilgrimage was a profound and life-changing experience. At the end of the fourth century, an Italian monk, Rufinus of Aquileia, recalled his stay in Egypt: 'When we came near, they realised that foreign monks were approaching, and at once they swarmed out of their cells like bees. They joyfully hurried to meet us.' Rufinus was deeply impressed by the solitude he found: 'This is the utter desert, where each monk lives alone in his cell … There is a huge silence and a great peace there.'[26]

Egeria

Egeria was probably a nun from a community in Galicia, in north-west Spain, who went on pilgrimage to the Near East in the 380s. Wishing to immerse herself in the Old and New Testaments, she travelled first to the Sinai desert, and continued to Jerusalem and then Constantinople. She wrote an account of her travels for her sisters back at home, part of which survives. A seventh-century Galician monk, Valerio of Bierzo, wrote a letter in praise of Egeria, urging others to copy her example. He describes the motivation for such a journey, for which Egeria prepared by studying the scriptures:

In the strength of the glorious Lord, she fearlessly set out on an immense journey to the other side of the world … First with great industry she perused all the books of the Old and New Testaments, and discovered all its descriptions of the holy deserts. Then in eager haste (though it was to take many years) she set out, with God's help, to explore them …

Sixth-century monastery of St Catherine, at the foot of Mount Sinai.

Moved by the longing for a pilgrimage to pray at [Sinai] the most sacred Mount of the Lord, she followed in the footsteps of the children of Israel when they went forth from Egypt. She travelled into each of the vast wildernesses and tracts of the desert which are set forth in the Book of Exodus.[27]

Egeria's own account of her pilgrimage survives in part, in a manuscript likely to have been copied by a monk at Monte Cassino in the eleventh century. She describes Mount Sinai, and the monks she met there:

Here then, impelled by our God and assisted by the prayers of the holy men who accompanied us, we made the great effort of the climb ... And when with God's help we had climbed right to the top and reached the door of [the] church, there was the presbyter, the one who is appointed to the church, coming to meet us from his cell. He is a healthy old man, a monk from his boyhood and an 'ascetic' as they call it here – in fact, just the man for the place. Several other presbyters met us too, and all the monks who lived near the mountain, or at least all who were not prevented from coming by their age or their health ...

Our way out took us to the head of this valley, because there the holy men had many cells, and there is also a church there at the place of the Bush (which is still alive and sprouting) ..., the Burning Bush out of which the Lord spoke to Moses, and it is at the head of the valley with the church and all the cells.[28]

Colour plate 1 depicts hermits' caves in Wadi Fayran, near Mount Sinai. Close by are the remains of a fifth-century monastery for women, where a few Orthodox nuns still live and pray.

Cassian

The most popular accounts of the Near Eastern monasteries were those of John Cassian, whose works became well known in Gaul, and also in Ireland. With a companion, Cassian set out for Egypt in about 385, and spent fifteen years learning from the monks and nuns whom he met. After a further twenty years of reflection on his experience, Cassian wrote his *Institutes* and *Conferences* for a monastery near Marseilles in about 425. In these books, he explained the aims and methods of monastic life; he helped western Christians to understand the life of eastern, Greek-speaking monks, and to adapt it to their own very different conditions. Cassian's Latin writings were circulated widely and were eagerly read.

Why the desert?

The Old Testament was very real for early Christians, who lived in a biblical landscape. Later monks and nuns entered the Old Testament through chanting the psalms and listening to the scriptures. They came to see themselves as God's Chosen People, and they developed a spirituality of the desert. They saw themselves as descendants of the children of Israel, rescued from slavery in Egypt, and led by Moses into the Sinai desert, where they came to know their God. He miraculously fed them on manna and quails (Ex. 16. 1-21) and quenched their thirst with water (Ex. 17. 1-7). For forty years, God slowly fashioned them into a faithful people, who would bind themselves to him by a covenant, in a relationship as close as marriage.

The Old Testament prophets return to this theme: over the years, Israel has grown unfaithful, but God will lead them back into the desert, where he will once more become their husband. Even today, when a Bedouin couple marry, they go out from their settlement into the desert, where the villagers will have prepared a hut with bread and milk. The newlyweds will honeymoon in seclusion, and if they stay in the desert longer than expected, the villagers will bring them more provisions.

Some time after 750 BC, the Prophet Hosea depicts God enticing Israel, his bride, back to the desert:

> I am going to allure her,
> and bring her into the wilderness,
> and speak tenderly to her …
> There she shall respond
> as in the days of her youth,
> as at the time when she came out of the land of Egypt.
> On that day, says the Lord,
> you will call me 'My husband' (Hos. 2. 16-18).[29]

To westerners the desert may be a hostile place, but to those who live there, it is home. For ancient Near-Eastern peoples, it was where one could honeymoon with God. The desert could be dangerous, but God was there. The evangelists depict Jesus preparing for his life's work by spending forty days in the Judean desert, recalling the forty years that the Israelites wandered in the wilderness. Here, Jesus not only struggled with demons; he also encountered God. Mark relates: 'The Spirit drove him out into the wilderness and he remained there for forty days, and was tempted by Satan. He was with the wild beasts, and the angels looked after him' (Mk. 1. 12, 13).

Eastern monks and nuns went out into the desert not only to fight with demons, but also to encounter God and be transformed by this intimate experience. In the fourth century, Bishop Athanasius of Alexandria described how

Antony of Egypt (*c.* 250–356) emerged, transformed, after twenty years alone in the desert: 'His friends broke down the door by force. Antony came out … radiant as though from some shrine where he had been led into divine mysteries and inspired by God'.[30] Western monks and nuns were motivated by the same desire as Antony and his friends: they chose an ascetical life in a deserted place in order to be irradiated by God.

Irish deserts

Desertum means 'an empty place', where a person could be alone with God. Ireland had no barren deserts like those inhabited by monks of the Near East, but there were always 'empty places' where a monk could find more time for solitary prayer. Early monks might establish a community and also build a hermitage for themselves at a more remote site, which became their *díseart*, or desert. 'Déclán's Desert' in Ardmore is in a sheltered spot beside a spring, on a headland at a distance from his monastery (*colour plate 2*); the foundation will be described more fully in Chapter 5. A century later, Kevin of Glendalough chose his Desert on rising ground above the Upper Lake at Glendalough, a mile to the west of his monastery (*colour plate 3*).

In 1969, E.G. Bowen plotted a distribution map of almost 100 Irish sites named *díseart* or *teampaill* (an early word for 'church'). Some sixty-five are concentrated in the third of the country which lies to the south of the great Central Plain. Bowen suggested a possible distinction between the great monasteries established by Finnian of Clonard in the Central Plain in the sixth and the seventh centuries, where fewer *díseart* sites are found, and the foundations close to the great rivers of the south, which might have received monastic ideas from Gaul at an earlier date.[31]

Castledermot

Díseart Diarmada, whose English name is Castledermot, was a monastery in Kildare which began as a hermitage established in 812 by a monk named Diarmaid, on the bank of the River Lerr, a tributary of the Barrow. Two fine high crosses and the base of a third survive at the site, carved in granite during the ninth century. Colour plate 4 depicts the east face of the north cross: its centre panel portrays Adam and Eve on either side of the tree of life. To the left, King David plays a harp as he chants the psalms which he composed: this is one of the few early depictions of an Irish harp. The image reminded the monks of their daily and nightly task of chanting the psalms. To the right, Abraham prepares to sacrifice his son, Isaac, foreshadowing the death of Christ on the cross.

The 'desert' theme is reflected on the panels of the high cross. In the central panel beneath the crucifixion scene on its west face, two of the Egyptian Desert Fathers, Antony and Paul the Hermit are depicted: a raven brings them a round loaf which they share. A panel at the base of the cross develops the theme, with a carving of the loaves and fishes which Jesus gave out

Antony and Paul the Hermit break bread, north cross, Castledermot, Kildare.

Geometric designs, south cross, Castledermot, Kildare.

to feed a multitude of hungry followers in the wilderness. Two similar panels feature on the east face of the south cross; its west face is covered with geometric designs.

Later attacks

There is a round tower near the centre of the enclosure, which is unusual in that it is situated to the north of the church instead of to the west, and because its entrance is raised only slightly above ground level; it was therefore vulnerable to attack. It is built of granite blocks and smaller pieces of limestone, and is capped by battlements of unknown date. There are a number of Celtic grave markers in the circular graveyard. The community had a troubled history: it was plundered twice by Vikings in the ninth century, and burnt in 1106. It appears that Vikings eventually settled here as Christians, for the graveyard contains the only Irish example of a Scandinavian hogback tombstone.

2

PATRICK AND
HIS FOLLOWERS

There were Christians in Ireland before the arrival of Patrick, but it is not known how strong their presence might have been, nor is it known how Christianity was brought to Ireland. While mainland Britain was largely Christianised simply by being part of the Roman Empire, Ireland developed rather differently. Britain's Roman towns had bishops, who exercised pastoral care over the Church in their area, and continued to do so after the departure of the Romans. Since Ireland was never under imperial administration, it had no urban bishops. However, it was considerably influenced by Roman culture, and Christians from the Roman Empire travelled to Ireland from early times.

Roman influence in Ireland

In the mid-second century, Ptolemy named locations in Ireland, implying that traders visited its shores and were familiar with its place names. A hoard of fourth-century imperial gold coins and Roman pendants, also of gold, have been found in the passage grave of Newgrange in Meath; such finds suggest that Romanised Britons settled in Ireland and were buried there. Most of these Roman artefacts have been found in Leinster, the kingdom closest to south-east Britain, and in north-eastern Ireland, which was only a day's sail from southern Scotland.

The Romanised families who settled in Ireland in the fourth century were probably traders who came from Britain and perhaps from Gaul. They would have controlled shipping and markets, and staffed establishments at the mouths of Ireland's navigable rivers, in order to obtain goods from further inland. They spoke Latin, and employed native Irish who probably needed to write a little and count in Latin. There may also have been Irish soldiers serving in auxiliary cohorts of the Roman army in Britain and elsewhere. These men would return home when they had finished their service.

Latin words entered the Irish language at this time, including such military terms as arms and soldier, tribune and legion, wall and longship. The royal seat of Cashel in south-east Ireland derives its name from the Latin word *castellum*, meaning a fort. Other fourth-century Irish words were borrowed from Latin by traders: purple-dyed cloth, dish and brooch, quill pen and oven, and even days of the week, Wednesday and Saturday.[1]

At this time, Christians used Latin in worship, and it is likely that a number of Irish people were competent Latin speakers, particularly in the southern kingdoms of Munster and Leinster. This is where the greatest number of ogham-inscribed memorial stones are found; some are inscribed both in ogham and Latin. The concept of incised commemorative slabs came from the pagan Roman Empire, and ogham probably pre-dates the arrival of Christianity in Ireland. The inventors of this cryptic alphabet were familiar with the sound values of spoken Latin; the language may have been devised by Latin-speaking Irish intellectuals, perhaps even as early as AD 300. The alphabet uses the sound values of spoken Latin and consists of incised lines grouped along two adjacent sides of a stone slab. Strokes were easier to carve than the rounded letters of the Latin alphabet.

An example of an ogham-inscribed stone can be seen in the chancel of the ruined cathedral at Ardmore, on the south coast, midway between Cork and Waterford. On the front face, an inscription reads up and then down, carved on two angles of the stone. It can be translated into Latin as: DOLATI LUGUDECCAS MAQI [...MU] COINETA SEGAMONAS.

Ogham-inscribed stone, Ardmore Cathedral, Waterford.

In 1945, R.A.S. Macalister concluded that it means 'Of Dolativix the smith, Lugud's son, tribesman of Nia Segamain'.[2] Smiths were valued members of Celtic society: they carved swords for war, elaborate jewellery for the high-born and cauldrons for food. Visible against the back edge of the stone in the photo, a second inscription intrudes upon the first. While the earlier one is pocked, this shorter inscription is chiselled, and reads: BIGA ISGOB ..., which in Latin would read UICI EPISCOPUS, referring to a local bishop buried beneath the stone.

Christian words enter the Irish language

By the early fifth century, British Christians had introduced Latin words into Irish, amongst which are *cresen* (Christian) and *domhnach* (church, from the Latin *dominica*). Throughout Ireland, particularly in the south, there are, as we have seen, places named *teampaill* (from the Latin *templum* or church) and *díseart* (from the Latin *desertum*, or desert). Monks are also likely to have lived at sites containing the name-element *uaimh* (cave), and some-times *inis* (island).

In names such as Kildare and Killarney, the name-element *cill* comes from the Latin *cella*, a word that described the huts or cells in which monks lived. Two thirds of the parishes with the prefix *cill-* are found in Leinster and Munster in the south-east, where there were monks. In Scotland, the name-element *kil-* is also common: Kilwinning, 25 miles south-west of Glasgow, means 'cell of Finnian' (perhaps the Irish monk, Finnian of Movilla).

Palladius

The chronicler Prosper of Aquitaine wrote that in AD 431, 'Consecrated by Pope Celestine, Palladius is sent as the first bishop to the Irish who believe in Christ'. Pope Celestine had already sent Germanus of Auxerre (d. 446) to Britain on two missions to combat the heretical teaching of the Briton, Pelagius. The bishops held a conference at Verulamium, 25 miles north-west of London, where Germanus visited the tomb of St Alban, gathering some earth from his grave to take back to his new church in Auxerre. It was prob-ably Germanus who recommended that Palladius, who may have been a deacon in his church at Auxerre, should go and work among the Irish 'who believe in Christ'.

According to a tribute paid to him by Pope Celestine I, and described by Prosper in his work on Cassian entitled *Contra Collatorem*, Palladius spent a long time among the Irish. There may have been many Christians in Ireland before the arrival of Palladius since, as we have seen, numerous Latin loan words, mostly Christian, had already reached Ireland through the British lan-guage, probably from Wales, as early as the fourth century.

Patrick

While Palladius was sent as an emissary from Rome for the specific reason of dealing with heresy, Patrick was a local fifth-century bishop. Two of his works have survived: his *Confessio* and an *Epistola*, a letter to the soldiers of the tyrant, Coroticus. They provide the only testimony to Patrick as an historical figure, although recent scholars have questioned the authenticity of some passages in the *Confessio* concerning his family of origin and his birthplace. The earliest surviving manuscripts of the two works date from the ninth and tenth centuries, but Muirchú drew on both sources for his seventh-century *Life of Patrick*.

Patrick's writings

Neither of Patrick's two surviving works provides satisfactory clues as to exactly where or when he lived and worked. Coroticus, to whom he wrote his *Epistola*, was a leader of British warriors, of uncertain date, who lived by slave-trading, perhaps in north-east Ireland, or perhaps in Ceredigion in south-west Wales, or Strathclyde in Western Scotland. The aim of the letter was to obtain the release of Christians who had been sold into slavery to the Picts by Irish pagans.

The *Confessio* is Patrick's declaration of the great works of God, for this Latin word is used in the Psalms and elsewhere to proclaim God's mighty deeds and his mercy.[3] Patrick therefore acknowledges the powerful works which God has achieved through him. We are told in the *Confessio* that Patrick's family had taken leadership in their local church for two generations. His father was a Roman *decurion*, or civic official, who also held office in the church as a deacon, while Patrick's grandfather was a priest. Patrick does not tell us where he was born: one possibility is Birdoswald on Hadrian's Wall; another is the area of western Scotland near Dumbarton, in the Romanised area south of the Antonine Wall. A slightly greater weight of probability suggests somewhere in the south-west: perhaps Cornwall or Wales.[4]

Patrick's conversion

In his *Confessio*, Patrick tells us that when he was sixteen he was captured by Irish raiders and taken to Ireland as a slave. He writes: 'When I had arrived in Ireland and was looking after flocks the whole time, I prayed frequently each day. And more and more, the love of God and the fear of him grew in me, and my faith was increased and my spirit enlivened. So much so that I prayed up to a hundred times in the day and almost as often at night. I even remained in the wood and on the mountain to pray. And – come hail, rain or snow – I was up before dawn to pray … I now understand this, that the Spirit was fervent in me.'[5]

This is the most powerful and moving account we possess of the call of an early British Christian to conversion, and to a monastic way of life. It led Patrick to choose exile as a pilgrim for Christ. After six years he escaped or was freed, and returned home to Britain. He trained as a priest, perhaps in Gaul. Patrick felt drawn to return to Ireland as a missionary, and eventually did so. On his arrival in Ireland, he suffered hardships and was criticised and ridiculed, but he persevered, and baptised many people.[6]

His vocation

The details of his life are difficult to decipher from the *Confessio*. We gather that he was baptised in Ireland rather than in his family home, perhaps because he did not believe in Christ until his conversion, or perhaps because of a sin which he committed as a fifteen-year-old.[7] When he escapes from slavery, he sets sail with pagans, and lands in a 'desert' where he remains for twenty-eight days; it is unclear whether this is in Britain or Gaul.

This experience recalls the ancient Israelites wandering in the desert; Patrick, like Moses, acts as the spiritual leader of the group, and leads them through the desert for four weeks, rather than four decades. The starving pagans ask Patrick to intercede with God to provide food and, at his prayer, a herd of swine appear, which they kill and eat.[9] A second account of his captivity may be a doublet of the first. He is called by a vision to Ireland: he hears 'the Voice of the Irish' who call to him 'from around the wood of Foclut which is close to the Western Sea',[10] perhaps in County Mayo.

Patrick describes his 'elders' who have authority over him, either as colleagues or superiors. In his absence, they hold a meeting in Britain to decide about his work. A friend to whom he confessed his teenage sin brings it up against Patrick and his activity in Ireland.[11] It is unclear whether this prevents Patrick from becoming a bishop, but by the time he writes the *Epistola*, Patrick relates that he is indeed a bishop.

His mission

Patrick was not a missionary in the modern sense of the word: early Christians understood mission quite differently. In his *Confessio*, Patrick tells us that he travelled to the far ends of the known world in order to bring Christianity to an alien people: 'I have gone where no one else had ever gone to baptise people, ordain clergy or complete people [in their faith] … so that even after my death I may leave something of value to the many thousands, my brothers and sisters, sons and daughters I have baptised in the Lord.'[12] Patrick also trained priests to care for these new Christians: 'Through me … everywhere clerics were ordained [to serve] this people who have but recently come to belief.'[13] Patrick describes how 'the Irish leaders' sons and daughters are seen to become monks and virgins of Christ. This, of course, is not to the liking of their fathers, and they have to suffer persecution and false accusation from their parents.'[14]

Patrick felt called to establish Christian communities and to train others to lead them: 'It is truly our task to cast our nets and catch a great multitude and crowd for God; and [to ensure] that there are clergy everywhere to baptise and preach to a people who are in want and in need.'[15] Patrick appears to have worked in central and northern Ireland, while other early bishops were preaching in the south.

His death

We do not know where or how Patrick died. Our only clues are found in his *Confessio*. Patrick writes: 'I was all set to go [to Britain], and wanted to go, for it is my homeland and where my family is – and [to] Gaul to visit the brethren and to see the face of my Lord's saints – God knows how much I wanted to do this.'[16]

It appears that Patrick had hoped to visit his friends, perhaps the monks of Tours or Lérins, but instead he remained at his difficult task in Ireland: 'Not a day passes but I expect to be killed or waylaid or taken into slavery or assaulted in some other way. But for the sake of the promise of heaven I fear none of these things.'[17] Patrick kept faithful to the initial call that he had received as a teenager: 'The one and only purpose I had in going back to that people from whom I had earlier escaped was the gospel and the promises of God ... And this is my declaration before I die.'[18]

Armagh

Patrick appears to have been based in the north-east, where the monks of Armagh later claimed him as the founder of their cathedral; they recorded stories about Patrick which may be based on fact or may simply be ecclesiastical propaganda to promote their patron saint. His seventh-century biographer, Muirchú, describes a dramatic confrontation between Patrick and the High King who lived at Tara, 25 miles north-west of Dublin. He relates how Easter that year fell on the same day as the great Celtic fire festival, when every fire had to be extinguished, until a new one was lit on Tara at dawn. Patrick gathered his followers on the nearby hill of Slane, 12 miles further north, to celebrate the resurrection of Christ by lighting the Easter fire. The furious king came to Tara and encountered Patrick, who then emerged victorious from a contest of magic with the king's bards.

Muirchú's theology

Muirchú linked Patrick with Tara at a time when the Church of Armagh was forging an alliance with the rising dynasty of the Uí Néill, who used the ancient capital of Tara as a symbol of their authority. Muirchú wished to place the conversion of Ireland within a theological context: as the Israelites were delivered from their slavery to the Egyptians in a single night, and as Jesus freed the waiting dead through his resurrection on Easter night, so his servant Patrick delivered Ireland from paganism through celebrating the Easter Vigil and lighting the paschal fire. Muirchú explains that the Irish had already been prepared for this. Their wise men, or magi (he uses the gospel word to describe them) had consulted their books and already knew that a powerful new teaching would come to supersede them.[19]

While there is no conclusive evidence that Patrick ever visited Slane, an early Celtic monastery associated with Bishop Erc was established on the hilltop. A saying attributed to Patrick runs:

Bishop Erc,
whatever he judged was rightly judged.
Whosoever gives a just judgement
shall receive the blessing of Bishop Erc.

The monastery had a round tower, which no longer survives. The Irish annals state that in 950 it was set on fire by 'foreigners from Dublin': these were Vikings. Bishop Erc's bell and staff were burnt, along with many people who had taken refuge in the tower, including the reader of the monastery. The present ruined church dates from the sixteenth century.

Ancient gravestones outside the church, Slane, Meath.

Patrick's followers

The followers of Patrick are controversial and somewhat mythical characters. Many churches claim to have been founded by Patrick and his disciples, although such claims are rarely historical. Among these churches, early sites are likely to include those whose names incorporate the Celtic word *domnach* since, as we have seen, this is an early Irish word derived from the Latin *dominica*, meaning 'that pertaining to the Lord'. The term pre-dates monastic life, and probably indicates a non-monastic church, of the kind established by Patrick. Scattered across northern Ireland are thirty churches with this name-element; they may indicate where Patrick and his first companions worked.[20]

A mile north-east of Navan on the N51, Donaghmore in County Meath is the site of an early monastery, with a well-preserved round tower and a ruined church. Its name means *Domnach Mór*, or 'great church'. Patrick was said to have founded a community at Donaghmore, and placed it in the care of a

monk named Cassán (the name derives from John Cassian), whose relics were venerated here. Its round tower was built in the eleventh or twelfth century. It has a round-headed doorway 12 feet above the ground; this made access difficult for intruders. A relief of the crucifixion is carved on its keystone. Christ's legs are twisted; a human head has been carved on either side of the architrave. There are the remains of a small church beside the tower, dating from the fifteenth or sixteenth century, and some early gravestones in the churchyard. The round tower was restored in 1841.

Door into the round tower, Donaghmore, Meath.

Patrick's carry-man

Clogher is an early monastic site associated with one of Patrick's followers named Aedh Mac Caírthinn, a man whose task, it is said, was to carry the ageing bishop over rough terrain, and to help him across rivers. Clogher is beside the River Blackwater in Tyrone, 18 miles south of Omagh, in the ecclesiastical province of Armagh. According to the *Tripartite Life of St Patrick*, written in about 830, Mac Caírthinn founded a monastery at Clogher when he could no longer carry his master. The *Life* relates that one day, while lifting Patrick over a difficult piece of ground, Mac Caírthinn groaned with pain. The two men realised that Mac Caírthinn was now too old to do this work; the carry-man asked if he might settle in one place. Patrick agreed, and sent him to Clogher.

The story may or may not be true, but Clogher is indeed an early site. The first reference to a Christian presence at Clogher is found in Adomnán's *Life of Columba*. Writing around 688, about 180 years after Mac Caírthinn's death, Adomnán describes what may have been a double community of monks and nuns, in the fifth of Columba's 'Miracles', entitled 'Of Maugin, a holy virgin, daughter of Daimen, who lived in Clogher of the sons of Daimen'.[21] Adomnán relates that Maugin stumbled on her way home from the oratory after praying the Office, and broke her hip; she prayed to Columba, who sent a monk named Lughaid to Clogher, in order to heal her. Adomnán's *Life of Columba* is a valuable early document, since it is the only surviving source to have been written before 720; most other early texts are preserved only through later copies.

Patron of Clogher

The late fourteenth-century *Salamanca Codex* contains a description of Mac Caírthinn's life and miracles: the codex was perhaps written to confirm and enhance the identity of Clogher diocese, and the account was probably read aloud in Clogher Cathedral on his feast day. The codex appears to reflect twelfth-century Church politics: Patrick was the saint of Armagh and Mac Caírthinn the patron of Clogher; the story of the two men emphasised the positive relationship between the two sees.

In various genealogies, Mac Caírthinn is mentioned as one of the *Muintir Phádraig*, the group of people including a cook and a bell ringer who accompanied Patrick on his mission. Mac Caírthinn would have been a man of unusual strength in order to be Patrick's 'carry-man', which was an important task. It may be no accident that Mac Caírthinn's feast day is recorded from early times as 24 March, the octave of St Patrick's feast day, while the Office for Mac Caírthinn's feast is the only one to survive from an Irish source. A reliquary called 'The great shrine of St Mac Caírthinn', altered over the centuries, survives as the *Domnach Airgid* in the National Museum, Dublin.

There is a ring fort on the hill above the monastic site at Clogher; its chieftain may have granted land to Mac Caírthinn in order to build a church.

South cross, Clogher, Tyrone.

There are two magnificent high crosses in the cathedral cemetery, dating from the ninth or tenth century, and a tall sundial in the cathedral porch, decorated with interlace panels. Dating from the tenth or eleventh century, it is one of only six to survive in Ireland; sundials were necessary to help monks maintain their ordered life of work and prayer.

Mochta

Another follower of Patrick was Mochta, who died in about 534. He is described in the *Life of Columba* by Adomnán as 'a Briton and a holy man, disciple of the holy bishop Patrick'.[22] Mochta was said to have first settled in Meath, but because of local opposition he moved northwards and established a monastery in a settlement named Louth. A small twelfth-century church survives in Louth, known as *Teach Naomh Mochta*, or Mochta's House. It is a two-storeyed chapel with a tall roof, of a type unique to Ireland, with a croft, or attic, set above an arched barrel vault; this design prevented the roof from collapsing inwards. A stairway leads to the upper floor beneath the roof.

Louth became a bishopric, and gave its name to County Louth. There are the remains of two medieval abbeys alongside Mochta's church: St Mary's Abbey, thought to date from 1148, and that of Saints Peter and Paul founded a couple of years earlier; only a section of its wall survives. Nowadays, Louth is only a village, 4 miles north of Ardee.

Mochta's House, Louth.

Assicus the hermit

A number of early saints established hermitages off the remote north-western coast of Donegal. Writing in the late seventh century, Patrick's biographer, Tírechán describes a metalworker named Assicus (*Tossach*), who was said to be Patrick's favourite disciple. Assicus may have lived as a hermit on Rathlin O'Birne Island, nearly a mile off the coast at Malin Beg, 10 miles south-west of Gleanncholmcille. Here, three well-preserved early groups of buildings and enclosures are centred upon what may have been the hermitage of Assicus.

Beside the well house, a slab carved with an equal armed cross and an elaborate wreathed *chi-rho* monogram may even be the work of Assicus, on account of its unusual design and its superior craftsmanship.[23] Tírechán relates that when the elderly Assicus had lived in his hermitage for seven years, his disciples forcibly removed him so they could care for him on the mainland, where he died.

Cashel

A late account relates how Patrick came to Cashel to visit the King of Munster, who agreed to be baptised. Cashel in Tipperary was the chief stronghold of the kings of Munster for 900 years. As we have seen, its name comes from *caisel*, an Irish word derived from the Latin *castellum*, meaning a circular stone fort.

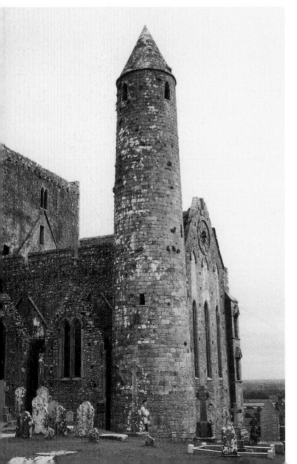

It is built on a rocky outcrop that dominates the surrounding land. Its first king was said to be Conall Corc, the son of a British mother who had returned from long exile in the land of the Picts. This may imply that Conall came from a group of Irish who had colonised parts of south Wales in about AD 400, and who were subsequently expelled. Conall or his brother and predecessor was the king whom Patrick is said to have baptised.[24]

It is not known how soon there was an ecclesiastical presence at Cashel, but a large church bell survives, dating from the ninth century. It is 12in high and 8in across, and is preserved in Limerick University. In 1101 the ruler of the

Round tower beside the cathedral, Cashel, Tipperary.

fortress handed over the Rock to the Church, as the seat of the new diocese of Cashel. New buildings were constructed, including a round tower, a cathedral and a magnificent chapel built by Cormac, King of Cork and Bishop of Cashel. Cormac's Chapel was consecrated in 1134.

St Patrick's cross

At this time, a magnificent cross, 7ft 6in high, was created in honour of Patrick. It is unique in that, instead of having a ring around the intersection of its shaft and transom, the weight of the cross was spread through two upright supports to its arms, one of which survives. These may have represented the crosses of the two thieves crucified on either side of Christ. There are indications of stone panels on each side of Christ's head, on which a pair of small angels may have been carved.

The crucified Saviour is depicted on what would have been the west face of the cross; he wears an ankle-length belted garment. On the east face is a robed bishop, who may represent Patrick: his feet rest on an ox head. The cross is tenonned into and supported by a massive base, which is said to have been the coronation stone of the kings of Munster. Its east side is decorated with interlaced beasts.[25]

Buite of Monasterboice

Buite Mac Brunaigh is described as a follower of Patrick, who founded Monasterboice
in Louth, near the east coast of Ireland; its
ruins are beside R168, 6 miles north-west
of Drogheda. The name Monasterboice (or
Mainistir Bhuithe in Gaelic) means 'Buite's
monastery'; it may have been founded at a
pre-Christian site. This is the only early Irish
place name containing the term *mainistir*,
meaning a monastery. We are told that Buite
established two separate communities of
monks and nuns, placing them widely apart to
protect their reputation.

Buite was described as a bishop who healed
many people. After his death in about 521,
the monastery became a significant centre of
learning. One of its most renowned scholars,
Flann, died in 1056. The Irish annals list the
deaths of twenty-two of its abbots between

West face of St Patrick's cross, Cashel, Tipperary.

759 and 1122, and mention a probable occupation by Vikings in about 968. They were expelled by Donal, High King of Tara, who, it is recorded, killed at least 300 Vikings in the process. The monastery remained in existence until 1122.

The round tower

The ruined round tower at Monasterboice is over 98ft high without its cap, one of the tallest in Ireland. Round towers were built in the ninth, tenth and eleventh centuries by monks throughout the country as defences against Viking attacks. They had no keystone for enemies to pull out, so they could not be demolished as speedily as conventional buildings.

Because of their height, round towers were excellent look-out posts. Since their doorways were normally several metres from the ground, a ladder could be pulled in when the monks were under attack. The only drawback was that if a burning arrow pierced the floorboards inside, the whole column acted as a chimney, and became a blazing inferno. When the round tower at Monasterboice was gutted by fire in 1097, much of the monastery's library and its church treasures were burnt.[26]

Muiredach's cross

Monasterboice boasts two of the finest high crosses in Ireland, both dating from the ninth century. Close to the round tower is the west cross, richly decorated with twenty-two panels depicting scenes from the Old and New Testaments. Near the entrance to the graveyard is the south cross, probably commissioned by Abbot Muiredach, who died at the monastery in 844; an inscription reads 'A prayer for Muiredach, by whom this cross was made'.

Punctuating the inscription are carvings of two cats: that on the left fondly licks her kitten, while that on the right clutches a bird which it has just killed. The principal theme of the cross is Christ, Lord of heaven and earth. Unusually, the crucified Christ

Crucifixion at the centre of Muiredach's cross, Monasterboice, Louth.

is depicted naked. Two angels support his head, so that it does not hang in symbolic defeat. The four sides of the cross are richly decorated with scriptural themes and abstract patterns.[27]

There is a third ruined cross in the north-east corner of the compound, which is believed to have been smashed by Cromwell's forces. Beside it is a granite sundial of uncertain date; within the enclosure there are also two ruined thirteenth-century churches. They probably had no connection with the monastery, which by then had ceased to function.

3

SOME ISLAND MONASTERIES

The few documents that tell us about Christian Ireland in the sixth century, in the hundred years after Patrick, describe monks, nuns and monasteries, rather than a church led by bishops, such as Patrick. A monastery is a place where one can learn holiness, and a place to practise what one is learning. It is also a garrison: it demarcates territory for God and holds off the enemy, Satan. It may be situated at the boundary between heaven and earth, on a hilltop such as St Catherine's Monastery on Mount Sinai, or on a rocky island close to the shore, such as Mont Saint Michel in France or St Michael's Mount in Cornwall.

A monastery is situated symbolically on the edge of the wilderness, at the boundary with dark powers; beyond the edge lies danger. Iona was established on the edge of civilisation, although within a hundred years it found itself at the centre of the Irish, Scottish and Northumbrian world. If training is important, a suitable training centre is crucial. A non-occupied space is helpful, although there were monasteries in cities. Under the guidance of someone experienced, one can learn holiness through practice. In the *Lausiac History*, Sophronius practised by going down to the shore to build, destroy and rebuild a hut of stones, as a sign that life is passing. This may have inspired western monks to build beehive huts of stone.[1]

Islands

An island forms a world of its own, cut off from the rest of the world; it was therefore considered a suitable location for a monastery. On an island, the training regime could be dominant, without interruption from the outside world. From the island, people might set off for even more isolated islands.

The ocean itself could be a training centre: the sailors form a monastery through rowing their boat, as in the *Voyage of Brendan*.[2]

In Classical antiquity, criminals were exiled to islands; early monks might live on islands as a self-imposed exile for the love of God. Yet Paradise was also thought of as an island where God dwelt, beyond the limitations of normal existence. Some of the first Irish monasteries were established on islands, the most important being that of Enda on the Aran Islands. This group lies in the Atlantic Ocean south-west of Galway, at distances of between 25 and 30 miles from the mainland. There are three principal islands: Inis Mór (9 miles long and 2 miles wide), Inis Meáin (3 miles by 2 miles) and Inis Oírr (4 square miles).

Enda's monastery

Since the Aran Islands lie so far out in the open sea, the weather can be atrocious: driving rains must have made monastic life quite difficult; however, the islands are low-lying, and storm clouds often pass over them, before breaking on the Galway coast. Another impediment to life in Enda's monastery was that Inis Mór (or 'Great Island') is barren limestone, which cannot support crops. Its topsoil is shallow, and largely artificial, having been created over the centuries by mixing sand from the shore with seaweed. It is too shallow to support trees, so wood for building monks' cells would have to be towed to the island. There is no wheat or straw, so even today, houses are thatched with reeds, which rot after a couple of years.

Enda (d. *c.* 530) was born in Meath on the Irish east coast, and was a soldier before becoming a monk. He is said to have founded monasteries in the Boyne valley, before taking his disciples to Inis Mór. The island had already been inhabited: on the south-west coast of Inis Mór is the great stone fort of Dún Aenghus, one of the largest prehistoric fortifications in Europe. There are two other stone forts on the island.

According to his *Life*, Enda was granted land where he established a monastery at Killeany (meaning 'cell of Enda') at the eastern end of the island. Many of the great Irish monks were said to have studied in Enda's monastery, of which all that remains today is the ruins of an eighth-century church known as *Teaghlach Eany*, (or 'Enda's household'). Enda is likely to be buried in the cemetery.

The church contains a fine eleventh-century cross shaft decorated with the figure of a horseman and interlaced patterns. There are remains of a tenth-century round tower, south of the cottages in Killeany; it was destroyed by Cromwell's forces in the seventeenth century. The tiny *Teampaill Benin*, also at Killeany, was founded by Beinin, possibly a contemporary of Patrick. It is oriented north–south, and may date from the seventh century.

Teampaill Mac Duach

North of Dún Aenghus, in the hamlet of Kilmurvey, *Teampaill Mac Duach* is dedicated to Colmán of Kilmacduagh (see Chapter 9), who founded one of the most important monasteries of Connacht at Kilmacduagh on the Galway mainland. *Teampaill Mac Duach* dates from the eighth to ninth centuries; its massive stone masonry and doorway with inclined jambs are typical of churches dating from this early period. Part of the embankment surrounding its enclosure is visible, and there is a tall cross-inscribed pillar outside the west door of the church.[3]

Teampaill Mac Duach, *Kilmurvey, Inis Mór, Aran Islands.*

The Seven Churches

Around AD 800 the Irish seem to have gone on pilgrimage to remote places in the country, including the Aran Islands, where later churches dedicated to Ciarán of Clonmacnoise and Kevin of Glendalough suggest that Aran was part of a wider pilgrimage network, which also included Clonmacnoise and Glendalough. Near the western end of Inis Mór, *The Seven Churches (Na Seacht d'Teampaill)* probably formed the most important pilgrimage site on Aran in medieval times. This is suggested by its name, which may derive from the circuit of pilgrimage churches on the Seven Hills of Rome; it is also known as *Díseart Breacáin*, or Brecan's Desert.

In medieval times, there may have been seven churches here, mostly of wood. Two stone churches survive, forming part of a series of structures with widely differing orientations, enclosed by a nineteenth-century wall. At the centre of the enclosure is *Teampaill Breacáin (colour plate 5)*, dedicated to Brecan, an obscure saint from Clare, whose dates are unknown, but who was probably a patron saint of the royal O'Brien dynasty of north Munster. It is large, and dates from the eighth to the thirteenth century, when it was extended, and a chancel arch was added.

Close by is *Teampaill an Phoill* ('the church of the hollow'), which dates from the fifteenth century, and is smaller and simpler in style. North of the churches are the ruins of rectangular houses, which may be the only pilgrim hostels to survive from late medieval Ireland. In the graveyards there are early crosses, including an elaborate knotwork cross; there are two holy wells, now covered over.

The Seven Churches: *early graveyard, Inis Mór, Aran Islands.*

Gobnait

The smallest of the Aran Islands is Inis Oírr; its name means 'island to the east'. Here, a small chapel is dedicated to a nun named Gobnait, who was born in Clare in the fifth century, and was said to have fled to the Aran Islands to escape a family feud. She eventually settled in southern Ireland, at Ballyvourney. There are remains of a cell and two bullaun stones at the early oratory on Inis Oírr. Bullaun stones are boulders with a hollow carved in them, whose function is unknown; they are often found at Irish monastic sites. They may be of pre-Christian origin, and were later perhaps used for grinding corn or containing water. Their name possibly derives from the Latin *bulla* ('a bowl') or the Gaelic *bullaun*, meaning 'a little pool'.

Also on the island, the *Church of the Seven Daughters* (*Cill na Seacht Níníon*) is said to be the burial place of seven sisters who were nuns. The dedication of two sites to nuns suggests that, in early times, this island was set aside for women. However, there is a also a holy well named after Enda (*Tobar Éinne*) on the island, and a small church dedicated to St Cavan or Kevin (*Teampaill Chaomáin*), which is usually covered by drifting sand; this is cleared once a year in order to hold a service at his tomb, to the north-east of the church. The commemoration takes place on Cavan's feast day, 14 June.

Senan's monastery on Scattery

Scattery Island, only half a square mile, lies in the mouth of the River Shannon, on the Clare side of the estuary. It can be visited on foot via a ferry which sails from the market town of Kilrush, a mile away. Senan therefore chose a monastic site which was much more accessible than Enda's on Aran. Since it was situated at the mouth of Ireland's longest river, it was vulnerable to attacks by Vikings, who plundered the monastery in 972, 1057 and 1101. However, it continued to thrive, and because of its location it grew wealthy by controlling maritime traffic. By the twelfth century, the tiny island had become a diocese in its own right.

Senan is thought to have lived in the first half of the sixth century. We learn about him from a thirteenth-century *Life* in Latin verse, from an earlier prose *Life* in Irish, and an account of his miracles. We are informed that he was born on the mainland at Magh Lacha (Moylougha), near Kilrush, and that he tended his father's cattle before becoming a monk. His monastic foundations include Inniscarra near Cork, Canon Island (also in the Shannon), Mutton Island off Seafield Harbour in Clare and Scattery Island; his feast day, 8 March, is recorded as early as the ninth century. His bell shrine can be seen in the Royal Irish Academy, Dublin.

East window, St Senan's church, Scattery Island, Clare.

St Mary's Cathedral and round tower, Scattery Island, Clare.

St Mary's Cathedral, showing massive lintel and antae, or projecting pillars, Scattery Island, Clare.

There were formerly seven churches on Scattery Island, but one has been eroded by the sea. *Teampaill Senain* ('Senan's church'), is a small, simple building dating from the twelfth century, with an east window splayed outwards, a unique architectural feature. A large stone slab set against the west wall of the church, now used as a seat, is inscribed with two letters of the ogham alphabet. To the west of the ruined church is Senan's Bed, a small chapel where he is said to be buried. A nearby early medieval cross slab requests a prayer for Moenach, tutor of Mugron.[4]

Teampaill Mhuire (St Mary's Cathedral) was built in the eleventh century. It has a doorway with a massive lintel, and distinctive *antae*, or short extensions of the side walls beyond the gable walls. These are a feature of early Irish churches, and were designed to support the roof timbers. To the west of the cathedral is a round tower, one of the oldest and tallest in Ireland, standing 85ft high. It was built in the tenth or eleventh century; its truncated cap may have been struck by lightning. Unusually, its entrance is at ground level, making it vulnerable to attack, and its doorway has inclined sides. Many pilgrims still visit the holy well, close to the round tower. It is known for its healing properties, and is associated with a pattern, or festival, held on Senan's feast day.[5]

Senan's encounter with Connera

The *Life of Senan* describes an interesting encounter between Senan and a young woman who begs to join him on Scattery, but is refused because of her sex. The account begins: 'A holy virgin, named Conegra, [Connera] led a most devout life in South Bantry ... At prayer in her cell one night after Matins, she saw the convents of Ireland in a vision, and Iniscahy [Scattery] was the nearest to heaven. She prayed to go there, and landed near the island. St Senan went out to meet her, and welcomed her, and told her to go a little to the east of his monastery, and join his mother and sisters. She replied: "I did not come to them, but to stay in your convent and serve God therein". Senan replied: "No women come on my island". She asked why, since Christ saved women as well as men, and died for them.'

Connera begs to receive the eucharist from Senan and asks for the place of her resurrection on the island. She thus seeks to live and die there. However, Senan replies: 'You shall have a burial place in the strand, but the tide may wash away your bones'. She asks him as a favour that 'You will out of charity cause a tombstone to be built over my body'. The site of Connera's grave ('Lady's Grave') is a small, former sand spit on the west shore of the island, visible on early maps, but now eroded by the sea. Since the spit was covered by the tide twice a day, it was considered to belong to the sea; therefore Senan did not violate monastic enclosure by allowing her burial on the strand.

Colum's monastery on Iniscealtra

Another early island monastery can be seen in Lough Derg, the largest lake in the River Shannon, on a tiny island in Scarriff Bay named Iniscealtra, or 'Church Island'. It is 20 miles north-east of Limerick, in Clare. Boat trips can be arranged from the East Clare Heritage Centre at Tuamgraney, 3 miles west of the island. Iniscealtra is surrounded by a number of ring forts on the mainland, a reminder that in early times this region was both well populated and fought over, although now it is idyllic and peaceful.

In the sixth century, Colum of Terryglass founded a monastery on Iniscealtra. At the highest point of the island is a D-shaped enclosure of about an acre, which was a ring fort.[6] This suggests that Colum was given the site for a church by the local chieftain. According to the *Acta Sancti Columbae de Tyre da Glass*, Colum found a lime tree on the island, 'whose distilled juice filled a vessel, and that liquor had the flavour of honey and the headiness of wine'. Lime blossom produces excellent honey, and the 'distilled juice' was probably mead, a fermented mixture of honey and water. The lime tree is not indigenous to Ireland, however, and so it is relatively rare.[7] Colum died in 548/9, of the so-called Yellow Plague that wiped out many Irish monks, spreading easily among men living in community. He was buried on Iniscealtra, but transferred to Terryglass seven years later.

Abbot Caimin

The monastery on Iniscealtra grew and developed under the leadership of Caimin (*c*. 600–54), who is described in the *Annals of the Four Masters* as attracting many disciples during his fourteen years as abbot. He was said to have many stepbrothers, including Colmán of Kilmacduagh. The monastery became known as a centre of learning, but from 836 onwards it suffered from Viking attacks. The *Annals of Innisfallen* record that in 922 the foreigners 'have thrown into the water its relics and shrines'. At the beginning of the eleventh century, the High King Brian Boru rebuilt some of the monastery, and his brother Marcan became its abbot.

A manuscript survives known as *The Psalter of St Caimin*, dating from the second half of the eleventh century: it is one of the finest of the later Irish manuscripts. The Psalter consists of six unbound folios of fairly thick parchment, containing the first sixteen verses of Psalm 118 according to the Latin Vulgate, with copious comments in the margins, and more between the lines of text. It is now preserved in the Library of the Franciscan Monastery, Merchant's Quay, Dublin.[8]

The monastery

Iniscealtra was a centre of pilgrimage from medieval times until the nineteenth century. There are six churches on the island, a hermit's cell, a round tower, graveyards and numerous enclosures. Parts of St Caimin's church may have

Round tower and St Caimin's church, Iniscealtra, Clare.

been built by Brian Boru. Its windows are constructed in various styles: semicircular, square-headed and also triangular – the only example in early Irish architecture. A simple archway leads to an ancient cemetery which is unique in northern Europe, in that its eighty recumbent slabs are still in position, most dating from the twelfth century. Almost all the tombstones are inscribed with crosses, and some twenty have inscriptions. The incomplete round tower is 79ft high, with a doorway 11ft from the ground.

To the south of Caimin's church is St Brigit's church (or 'Baptism church'), with a fine west doorway: this is a small Romanesque structure, erected during a period of intensive building activity in the twelfth century (*colour plate 6*). It stands within an enclosure which is entered from the west through an elaborate doorway. Three sides of its surrounding wall were constructed during excavation by Liam de Peor in the 1970s, replacing a bank of earth and stones. Excavation inside St Brigit's church revealed that it was used for burials by the lay community on the island in the thirteenth century. Men, women and children were buried here; there were two graves of women who died in childbirth. East of Brigit's church is the larger church of St Mary, and nearby, on the eastern shore of the island, is St Mary's well.

An early shrine

A paved way leads to a small enclosure, containing a small shrine, described in the nineteenth century as a 'confessional'. It was restored many times, and dates from 1700 in its present form. It is rectangular, divided inside by enormous inclined jamb stones, which allow access to a square stone box-like structure. This may have been a slab shrine of the kind which enabled people to touch the relics of the buried saint. In the ninth or tenth century, a recumbent stone cross slab was placed on the same axis, with a slot to carry a second cross slab. Beyond this, on the same axis, is the hollow base of a high cross.

Inclined jamb stones over the early shrine, Iniscealtra, Clare.

Foundations for a high cross and cross slab at the shrine entrance, Iniscealtra, Clare.

This may have been the heart of the monastery: the grave of a holy person, which became a place of pilgrimage.[9] In 1976, Liam de Peor excavated this area and found that the 'confessional' had replaced a timber structure. He also discovered the remains of a mud-walled oratory nearby, which he dated to the seventh or eighth century.[10]

There are remains of four high crosses; an inscription in Irish on the base of one of them reads: 'the grave of the ten men'. It may refer to warriors who died while defending the monastery. At various places on the island are five bullaun stones, each with a hollow carved into it. On the ridge at the top of the site, there is a cemetery for children.

Skellig Michael

There were many other island monasteries both on lakes and around the Irish coast; perhaps the most dramatic is Skellig Michael (*Sceilg Mhichíl*). The Skelligs are two rocky islets, 9 miles west of Bolus Head on the Inveragh peninsula in Kerry; their name probably derives from *Na Sceallaga*, 'the Rocks'. Perched on a peak 525ft above the Atlantic Ocean, Skellig Michael is one of the most complete Irish monasteries dating from Celtic times. There are remains of at least six beehive huts standing close together, two square stone chapels and a ruined church, built on terraces on the sloping rock. A second more remote hermitage has been discovered on the higher south peak.

The windowless huts have walls 6ft thick; most of their roofs are still intact. They have survived because of the mild climate here, with its lack of frost. It is thought that stones protruding from the roof of the largest hut were used to anchor protective sods or thatch.[11] A few artefacts have survived from the monastery, including a small bronze figure of Christ on the cross, wearing a crown and a kilted tunic, about 4in high.[12]

There are some sixty carved crosses, grave markers and two wells on the island. The early monastery is reached by a flight of 1,670 stone steps leading up from the sea; the site is immediately above the landing place. In 2009, the archaeologist Michael Gibbons discovered a previously unknown stairway hewn into the solid rock, which represents a challenging ancient pilgrim route around the island. Gibbons also discovered a cross hewn in the rock, one of only a handful in Ireland.

Viewed from the sea, Skellig Michael looks like a secular fortification; we do not know whether this was symbolic, or whether this design derives from the fact that many monasteries were once chieftains' strongholds, or abandoned fortresses.[13] In Irish monasticism, monks founded monasteries in abandoned prehistoric forts because their model, St Antony of Egypt, had done so.[14]

The island may have supported about ten to twenty monks. There is little soil on Skellig Michael; it is thought that the monks brought topsoil from the mainland to create small gardens in which they could grow vegetables. The community was raided by the Vikings in the ninth century, and life on the rock was so harsh that eventually in the twelfth century the monks moved to Ballinskelligs on the mainland. In his novel *Sun Dancing: A Medieval Vision*, Geoffrey Moorhouse has reconstructed life in this remote monastery.[15]

4

BRIGIT AND OTHER NUNS

I n the fourth century, both men and women followed St Antony into the Egyptian desert, where some established communities. In Celtic Ireland, a similar pattern emerged: Patrick's biographer, Tírechán, describes small Christian centres which Patrick founded and left in the care of 'three brothers and a sister' or 'two young women' or even one woman. This pattern may not date back to Patrick's lifetime, and since Irish laws rarely allowed women to own land or pass it on, many of the small groups of nuns scattered around Ireland have left no trace. A nun might be given land for a monastery only for her lifetime; when she died, her followers dispersed and the land reverted to the men in her family who had given it to her.[1]

In the previous chapter we heard of Connera's attempt to join a monastery of monks, while Senan tried to persuade her to join his mother and sister, who also lived a vowed life. We also met St Gobnait, who fled to the Aran Islands to escape a family feud. Both stories suggest that women might have to struggle in their search for vowed life. Yet our earliest surviving Irish text, Patrick's *Confessio*, describes a flourishing Church with many women, both virgins and widows, accepting a call to live for God. He relates how one woman received her religious vocation soon after he had baptised her, and so he established her in this new lifestyle. He writes:

The Irish leaders' sons and daughters are seen to become the monks and virgins of Christ. Indeed, on one occasion this happened. A blessed Irishwoman of noble birth, a most beautiful adult whom I had baptised, came back to us a few days later for this reason. She told us how she had received a divine communication from a messenger of God which advised her to become a virgin of Christ and that she should move closer to God.

Thanks be to God, six days after that, she avidly and commendably took up that life which is lived by all virgins of God. This, of course, is not to the liking of their fathers, and they have to suffer persecution and false accusation from their parents. Yet despite this, their number keeps increasing, and we do not know the number of those born there from our begetting – apart from widows and those who are celibate.[2]

This provides us with valuable information. First, it is the earliest British account of a woman's call to single vowed life. Her parents would understandably be upset at the loss of a marriageable daughter, who could have enabled a useful tribal alliance with a neighbouring prince. Secondly, we learn that the vocation to celibate life could happen very soon after baptism. In the Syrian Church during the first three centuries, baptism was very thoroughly prepared for and celibacy was often vowed at baptism.[3] There seems to be an echo of this situation in Patrick's account.

Thirdly, we are told that this woman was highborn; she was therefore likely to be able to assume leadership in the local community of new Christians. Fourthly, Patrick tells us that he considered the presence of virgins and widows in the Church to be so important that he apparently kept a record of them, for he writes that he has no idea how many people he has baptised, but he does know how many celibates and Christian widows there are. At this time, when girls married at the age of puberty, 'virgins' would have been teenagers, and Christian widows, with a little more life experience, are likely to have assumed responsibility for them.

Women take the veil

These women would have dressed appropriately to their new state. In early Greek tradition, holy women prayed and prophesied with unbound hair,[4] whereas in the Judeo-Christian tradition, women wore veils, as St Paul emphasised when addressing the women of Corinth (1 Cor. 11. 4-16). The earliest evidence for this custom is in the Book of Enoch, a Jewish commentary on the Book of Genesis, written in about 100 BC. Its author recalls how in Genesis 6. 4, the giants came down and had sex with the [golden-haired] daughters of men; he therefore prescribes that women should cover their heads to protect themselves against demons.[5] According to this theology, the veil was a sort of safety helmet, in order to keep demons out of nuns' living space, to prevent Satan from being enticed into the monastic enclosure.

Brigit of Kildare

The most famous Irish nun was St Brigit, who is believed to have been born near Kildare, some 30 miles west of Dublin, where she later founded what became a large double monastery of monks and nuns. She lived a couple of generations after Patrick, and perhaps died around 525. Her community came to hold jurisdiction over a large part of south-west Ireland until the suppression of the monasteries. An early Irish *Life of Brigit* describes her travelling around the countryside in a chariot. Its driver was a priest who could baptise the people to whom they preached. Kildare means 'church of the oak': Brigit appears to have established her community beside this holy tree, which survived until the tenth century. The monastery soon grew in importance, and Brigit's early *Lives* were written to enhance its fame.

Cogitosus

In about 650 Cogitosus, who was probably a monk of Kildare, wrote a biography of Brigit that provides us with a valuable description of the monastery a hundred years after Brigit's death. He tells us of an elaborately decorated wooden church which contained the shrines of Brigit and Conleth, a hermit and metalworker whom Brigit invited to make church vessels for the monastery, and to be pastor of the surrounding people. The two shrines, one to the left and the other to the right of the altar, were adorned with precious metals and gems. There were crowns of gold and silver hanging above them, and the church also contained images, paintings and partition walls made of boards. Brigit's relics were still venerated when Kildare was raided by Danes in 836.

Cogitosus' *Life of Brigit* may well be the earliest surviving *Life* of an Irish saint. It appears to predate both Adomnán's *Life of Columba* and Muirchú's *Life of Patrick*; Muirchú refers to him as 'my [spiritual] father Cogitosus'.[6] The earliest manuscript copy of his *Life of Brigit* dates from the tenth century; unlike most Irish *Lives*, it is not a chronological story, but a series of themed miracles, on the model of Severus' *Life of Martin of Tours*.[7] The *Life* is a polished work of political propaganda: Cogitosus says that Kildare is the head of all the Irish churches, from coast to coast.

Other *Lives* of Brigit

There are two more *Lives* of Brigit, a long one perhaps dating from the mid-eighth century, and a brief *Irish Life* (*Bethu Brigte*). In the first of these, Brigit travels more than she does in the *Life* by Cogitosus but, significantly, Kildare is not claimed to be the chief church of all Ireland. While Cogitosus has the dynastic interests of north Leinster at heart, the other two *Lives* are more concerned with Ireland in general. They contain more magical elements; they depict Brigit meeting St Patrick, and relate how she was made a bishop by accident, the presiding bishop being drunk. The abbess of Kildare was powerful:

at the Synod of Kells/Mellifont in 1152, the abbess of Kildare took precedence over bishops.[8] Brigit, however did not have priestly powers; she needed to have a priest with her to baptise converts.

Ultán's Hymn

Brigit is honoured in one of the oldest hymns in the Irish language, perhaps dating from the seventh century. *Ultán's Hymn* combines pagan and Christian motifs to present Brigit as a woman associated with fire and the sun; she is also described symbolically as the mother of Jesus. The first half of the hymn runs:

> Brigit, woman ever excellent, golden, radiant flame,
> Lead us to the eternal kingdom, the brilliant, dazzling sun.
>
> May Brigit guide us past crowds of devils,
> May she break before us the attack of every plague.
>
> May she destroy within us the taxes of our flesh,
> The branch with blossoms, the mother of Jesus.
>
> The true virgin, easy to love, with great honour,
> I shall be forever safe with my saint of Leinster.[9]

Kildare monastery

Little survives of the Celtic monastery at Kildare except the remains of a high cross and a round tower. Just south of the thirteenth-century cathedral, the foundations of a small rectangular building were uncovered in 1996. Now named the Fire Temple, this may have contained the convent's communal hearth; a street beside the cathedral is named Fire Temple Lane. When Gerald of Wales visited Brigit's convent in the twelfth century, he saw a fire which the nuns carefully tended. He wrote: 'the fire is surrounded by a circular withy hedge, which men are not allowed to enter.' Brigit perhaps owes her name to Brígh, a Celtic goddess of fire and light, and inherited some of her attributes.

Kildare Cathedral is set on a low ridge where six roads meet, and Brigit's monastic 'city' became a large one. Cogitosus noted that the king's treasury was in Kildare, and the cathedral must have been worth plundering, for it was raided by Vikings sixteen times. Kildare seems to have been singled out for its wealth, for it was pillaged more frequently than other Irish monasteries. This suggests a steady flow of pilgrims, who donated generous gifts to Brigit's shrine. Gerald of Wales describes a fine illuminated manuscript which he called the *Book of Kildare*; it no longer survives.

Carved stone fragment, c.tenth-century, Kildare Cathedral.

Brigit's holy well, Kildare

One of the ancient roads leading to Kildare passes through Tully, a mile south of the city. Here is Brigit's well, and the site of the convent's watermill. There is no stream in Kildare, and running water was necessary to turn a mill wheel, in order to grind the community's flour. The well is still a place of pilgrimage; it can be found off a signed road opposite the Irish National Stud. Brigit's well is at the far end of a small meadow; its water flows through a pool, where a stone trough and seats on either side allow pilgrims to bathe. Beside the well, a larch tree is hung with clouties, symbolic of prayers for healing.

Brigit's well, Tully, Kildare.

'Clootie' or 'cloot' is a Scottish word for a rag or a strip of cloth. It is an ancient pre-Christian custom to hang clouties from trees beside a holy well in England and Ireland, as a request for healing, or in gratitude for a cure, but the custom is much more widespread. One can find clouties at holy wells beside rural Orthodox monasteries in Crete, for example, and across Asia, Africa and South America.

A closer look at the cloutie tree beside Brigit's well in Tully indicates the kinds of cures for which she is invoked today: bandages and handkerchiefs, socks and stockings, and children's toys form silent prayers for healing broken limbs, crippled feet and sick children. Brigit became a patroness of healers, midwives and newborn babies. She was also invoked to protect cattle and to bless their milk; in medieval iconography, a cow lies at Brigit's feet. In a culture in which childbirth could be hazardous, Brigit was often invoked to aid a healthy delivery. Because she was invoked in childbirth, a story arose that she was Mary's midwife at the birth of Jesus. Brigit was invoked as 'aid-woman of Mary' and 'foster mother of Christ'. In ancient cultures, midwives were highly honoured, and fostership was considered a close and tender tie.

Brigit, the goddess

In his *Glossary*, dating from the ninth century, a monk named Cormac recorded a belief that there was a pagan goddess of poetry named Brigit, who had two sisters with the same name: 'Brigit, i.e. a learned woman, daughter of the Good God [or *Dagda*]. That is Brigit, woman of learning, i.e. a goddess whom poets [*filid*] worshipped ... Her sisters were Brigit, woman of healing and Brigit, woman of smithwork – daughters of the *Dagda*, from whose names among all the Irish a goddess used to be called Brigit'.[10]

This appears to relate to Brígh, the goddess whose festival of Imbolc was celebrated on the first day of February, at the time when ewes come into milk. This became Brigit's feast day, a date associated with her from early times. It may be that, uniquely, the saint's cult spread to all Celtic regions because there was a pan-Celtic deity with her name. She was often associated with milk: in an Irish custom recorded on her festival, the wooden spoon for stirring the butter churn was addressed as 'Little Bride'. It was clothed in a child's dress and decorated with a straw cross called 'Little Bride's star'. Pins and needles, crystalline stones and pieces of straw were offered to Little Bride as gifts, and mothers brought her food.[11]

Brigit's cross

The custom of fashioning Brigit's cross out of rushes is widespread and ancient. A story to explain its origin relates that Brigit was called to the bedside of a dying pagan chieftain. As she sat beside him, she picked up some rushes from the floor and began to weave them into a cross. He watched her and asked what she was doing, and she told him the story of the crucifixion. Before he died, the chieftain was converted and baptised. Crosses are fashioned on St Brigit's day and put in the rafters of homes, to protect them from harm throughout the year. However, Brigit's cross is likely to pre-date Christianity, since its earlier form has three arms, not four. Brigit's cross is often hung over the byre to bless the cows, since Brigit was the patroness of cattle, as was Brígh before her. The Celts were a pastoral people, and cattle were precious possessions.

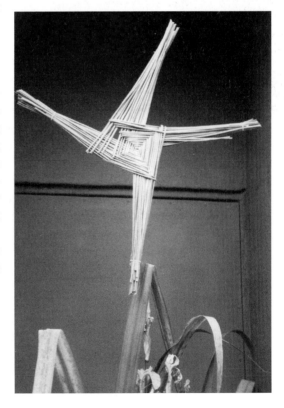

Brigit's cross, Tully, Kildare.

The woven cross of rushes is an Irish variant of the corn dolly: in regions where it is difficult to grow corn, rushes are used instead. The corn dolly is a shrine in which the corn spirit was seen to reside as a life-giving presence in the home. The word 'dolly' (or 'little idol') is an ancient name for an image or representation. Throughout Europe and the Near East, corn dollies of various designs have been hung in homes, barns and churches, as a symbol of blessing and a prayer that crops will flourish.[12] Brigit's connection with the fertility of crops, cattle and children is another indication of the fusion of her cult with that of a pre-Christian goddess.

Nevertheless, post-medieval oral tradition concerning Brigit in Ireland and Scotland does not necessarily imply that traditions surrounding Brigit evolved from that of a goddess. It is difficult to assess pagan material, recorded in the Christian period, written largely within a monastic context; perhaps female saints were considered more 'pagan' than male saints. Brigit emerges as a humble, likeable person, who provided the poor with food and milk, and yet, although the texts describing her are relatively early, we cannot glimpse Brigit the person, but only other peoples' ideas of who she might have been.

Darlugdach of Abernethy

Brigit has many dedications across the Celtic world and in mainland Europe, including various Scottish Kilbrides and numerous Welsh Llansanffraids ('church of St Bride'). There are a few foundations connected with her early followers, including Abernethy, 6 miles south-east of Perth, in eastern Scotland. According to the *Pictish Chronicle*, St Bride's church at Abernethy was founded in the sixth century. A note upon the chronicle relates that when King Nechtán was driven from his land by his brother Drust, he visited Brigit's monastery in Kildare, to ask for prayers. Nechtán was restored to his kingdom, and three years later Darlugdach, Abbess of Kildare, came to Britain as an exile for Christ. After a further two years, Nechtán offered Abernethy to God and St Brigit. During the Mass of consecration, Darlugdach 'sang Alleluia over the offering'.[13]

Abernethy became the principal seat of the southern Picts, with a Celtic bishop. In about 590, some of Columba's monks rebuilt Abernethy's wooden church in stone, with the blessing of Gartnaith, King of the northern and southern Picts. The scene changed, however, when another Nechtán became King of the Picts in 706. He declared his allegiance to Rome and expelled the Columban monks from Abernethy, since they followed the Celtic tradition. After his death, Abernethy once more became the Pictish capital.

In the eighth century, we hear of St Donald's nine daughters entering St Bride's monastery, which appears to have been a double community. In the following century, Abernethy's bishop, Adrian (d. 875), an Irish missionary, was killed by Vikings on the Isle of May in the Firth of Forth. In the tenth century, perhaps as a defence against the Vikings, an Irish-style round tower was built beside the church, one of only two in Scotland. A Pictish symbol stone beside the tower depicts a hammer, anvil and tongs; it is the earliest surviving feature at the site.

Pictish symbol stone, St Bride's monastery, Abernethy, Fife.

St Íte

Unlike Brigit, Íte was an ascetic; she was a patron saint of Munster. The sources for her life are later than Brigit's, and equally problematic. Íte founded a monastery at Killeedy (or 'cell of Íte'), 20 miles south-west of Limerick, which may have been a double one; its nuns disappeared early on, but death notices of its abbots survive. She was patroness of the Uí Conaill Gabra who, according to the *Annals of Ulster*, won a victory at her intercession in 552. However, another source, the *Laud Genealogies*, claims that the opposing, weaker, side won as a result of her prayers; they are likely to have 'owned' her as their patron first.[14] The *Annals of Ulster* record Íte's death in 570 or 577.

Íte's *Life* dates from the eleventh century, but her miracles seem to have been recorded within two generations of her death. She is said to be one of the Déisi of Munster, a chieftain's daughter who was baptised Deirdre (or Dorothea in Latin), and subsequently nicknamed Íte, or 'Thirst [for God]'. According to her *Life*, she was born in Waterford in the south-east, subsequently moving westwards to Limerick: there are many dedications to her in both areas.

She is described as the *matrona* of the Uí Conaill Gabra, while Senan of Scattery Island, whom we met in the previous chapter, was their *patronus*, or legal protector. We are told that she refused marriage, against her father's wish. She therefore took the legal action of fasting against him,[15] the equivalent, perhaps, of going on hunger strike. Fasting is a theme in Íte's life: God sends her an angel who asks her to moderate her fasts, but Íte refuses, so God provides her with heavenly food. She runs a small school of saints, or is their mentor; at her burial she is described as 'a second Brigit in her virtue and habits'.

Íte's 'beetle'

The earliest reference to Íte is an Old Irish four-line poem in the *Martyrology of Óengus*, dating from about 800. It notes her feast day as 15 January, and comments:

> She succoured many grievous diseases;
> She loved many severe fastings,
> The white sun of Munster's women,
> Íte the devout, of Cluain.[16]

A later commentary in Middle Irish is attached to the first line of this text, dating from the twelfth century; we are unsure whether it conveys a widespread belief or that of an individual. Offering a literal interpretation of the first verb of the quatrain, 'succoured', the commentary explains that a *dael* (perhaps to be translated as 'beetle') the size of a lapdog sucked at Íte and destroyed her entire side. Íte's parasite appears to conflate the concept of a leech, or worm which sucked blood and was used medically in the ancient world, with St Paul's statement about a thorn in his side: 'I was given a thorn in the flesh, an angel of Satan to beat me, and stop me from getting too proud' (2 Cor. 12. 7-9).

The commentary continues:

> No one knew that was happening to her. Once she goes out. The *dael* comes out of its den in her absence. The nuns see it and kill it. Then she returns, and as it did not come, she asked, 'Where has my fosterling gone', she said, 'and who has interfered with it?' 'Do not deprive us of heaven,' said the nuns, 'it is we who killed it, for we did not know but that it was harmful'.[17]

Íte replies that because of their deed, none of them will succeed her. She begs God to give her his own Son to nurse, in place of the beetle. A tender poem follows, which may not have originally referred to Íte, since it does not name her. In charming, informal language, it describes Ísucán, which could perhaps be translated as 'dear little Jesus', since the suffix *-cán* is an intimate diminutive. The poem begins:

> Ísucán is in fosterage with me
> in my little hermitage …
> Jesus with the men of heaven
> against my heart every night.[18]

Like the fosterling beetle, Christ the fosterling now feeds at Íte's breast. Paradoxically, the poem contains numerous legal terms to describe Íte's relationship with Jesus, her foster child. It employs the language of entitlement: since Íte is Christ's foster mother, he owes her various 'sound contracts' but, on the other hand, he is almighty God. This is a successful composition by a poet who loves God, enjoys word play and understands legal terminology.[19]

St Attracta

This nun is named in Latin sources as Attracta, meaning 'She who is drawn to Christ'; in Irish she is named Aracht or Adhracht. The concept behind her name comes from the Song of Songs in the Old Testament, in which the bride sings: '… the maidens love you. Draw me in your footsteps, let us run.' (Song of Songs 1. 3). According to her legend, she ran away from home and received the veil from St Patrick at Coolavin, but it is more likely that she lived after Patrick's death, in the sixth or seventh century. Several churches and holy wells are dedicated to her in Galway and Sligo. Attracta is said to have founded a hospice for travellers at a place now called Killaraght in her honour; the hostel survived until 1539, and a nearby well is named after her. She was known for her healing powers; her brother was a monk named Connell.

One of the more interesting sites dedicated to Attracta is at Kiltura in Sligo. Kiltura is set in farmland, 5 miles south-south-west of Bunnaddan, and 14 miles south-south-west of Sligo. The village and its church no longer survive, except for a 'Famine Graveyard' and Attracta's holy well, half a mile away, which is within a ring barrow, above the west bank of a stream. Attracta was a local saint whose feast was celebrated here until recently, when pilgrims visited her well and the hawthorn trees that encircled the barrow.

Attracta's holy well is a tiny artificial inlet leading from the stream. Grouped around the well are a pillar stone, a nineteenth-century memorial slab to the Cooke family, a holed stone and a cross-inscribed stone (*colour plate 7*). The eastern side of the barrow falls away into the water. The holy well and stones are on the south-east side of the barrow, which has a raised central platform; its earthen bank is visible in places.[20] In summer, delicate pink spotted orchids and other wild flowers grow at the site.

The inscribed pillar stone is the earliest monument at the site: it stands 22in

high and is carved from sandstone, decorated with a plain ringed cross. Eight vertical lines project upwards from its cross bar: the carving might represent two mythical animals, while others suggest that this could be 'c c' in ogham. Beside it is the Cooke memorial stone, and a large slab of purple sandstone with a hole through it, which may have acted as an agreement stone, where contracts or pledges of loyalty were made by joining hands through the hole and swearing on it. Such stones are also known as Marriage Stones, where couples would promise fidelity while clasping hands through the stone.[21] The fourth stone is a plain cross-incised slab of uncertain date.

Sandstone pillar, St Attracta's well, Kiltura, Sligo.

To find Attracta's well, take the R294 west from Gorteen. Turn left straight after passing 'Sligo Farm Services', on the left. Continue along the road, which becomes a grassy track, and over a small bridge. At a sign pointing left to Kiltura Cemetery, follow the road right, to the nearby farm. In the stableyard, go through the gate into the field on the left; the well is down to the right. Or ask at Holy Well View Cottage, on the left round the next corner.

5

EARLY SAINTS OF MUNSTER

Munster and Armagh

The medieval *Lives* of at least four Munster saints claim that they preached the gospel and founded monasteries before the arrival of Patrick in Ireland. They include bishops Déclán of Ardmore, Ailbe of Emly, Ciarán of Saighir and Abbán of Moyarney; however, these claims are to be treated with caution, since their authors were partly motivated by Church politics. As early as the seventh century, Armagh was promoting the cult of Patrick, claiming that he brought Christianity to the island, and chose Armagh as his principal foundation. By presenting him as the apostle and first bishop of the Irish, scholars at Armagh, particularly Tírechán and Muirchú, sought to establish and control a network of religious houses throughout Ireland.[1] As we have seen, Tírechán claimed that Munster was converted when Patrick arrived at Cashel and baptised its chieftain.

The authors of the *Lives* of the early saints of Munster attempt to challenge this view. They do not deny the national importance of Patrick; instead, the *Life of Ailbe* describes Ailbe as a 'second Patrick and patron of Munster', and relates how Patrick entrusted Munster to him. A number of the *Lives* of Munster saints, including a *Life of Ailbe* under his German name, Albert, were composed in the 1160s or 1170s at Regensburg and in other Irish Benedictine monasteries of southern Germany, many of whose monks came from Munster; kings of Munster gave generous donations to these foundations.[2]

Déclán of Ardmore

The chief source for Déclán's life is a twelfth-century Latin *Life*, in which he is presented as a Munster saint who preceded Patrick; he is described as a bishop of the Déisi of east Munster. This appears to reflect the political ambitions of his monastery at Ardmore, when the Irish Church adopted a new diocesan system. Ardmore hoped to become the seat of a new diocese, but instead, this was conferred upon Lismore, which had been founded by St Mochuda.[3]

Déclán's impeccable credentials are described: he travels to Rome, and is ordained bishop by the pope. Here he meets his fellow Munster bishop, Ailbe of Emly, and on returning to Ireland, he meets Patrick. Throughout the text, Déclán recognises the supreme authority of both these figures; Patrick instructs him to found a monastery at Ardmore, and with Patrick's blessing, he converts the Déisi to Christianity.

However, his enthusiastic biographer extends Déclán's life span dramatically: in Chapter 15, he meets David of Wales, who lived a hundred years later, in the sixth century, while St Ultán of Ardbreccan, who died in the seventh century, is presented as his pupil. Later, Déclán visits the Déisi who live further north in Meath, where the king of Tara welcomes him and grants him land in order to found a 'monastery of canons'. This is twelfth-century language: canons were appointed to serve cathedrals. The historical Déclán perhaps lived in the sixth century.

Déclán's life

The *Life of Déclán* relates that he was a prince of the Déisi, a tribe which had been expelled from Tara;[4] the story of their wanderings was told by the Irish bards. Some of the clan returned to Tara, some migrated to Wales, and others found a home in south-east Ireland, after an intertribal marriage. Here, Déclán was born: according to his *Life*, there were already Christians in the area, and a priest named Colmán came to his parents' home and baptised their son. Following Celtic custom, Déclán was fostered by his uncle. At the age of seven he was sent to a holy man, and learnt to read, write and pray. Déclán also went abroad to study, perhaps to Wales or Gaul, and returned with his monk's bell and staff.

Déclán established a monastery at Ardmore on the south coast, halfway between Cork and Waterford. *Ard mór* means 'great height', and Déclán chose a site on fertile high ground overlooking a sandy bay. The headland may then have been an island in the mouth of the River Blackwater, before it burst its banks in 803 and made a new channel to the sea through Youghal Bay. A cluster of Roman and early Christian remains has been found in the Blackwater valley, including a number of ogham-inscribed stones. From his monastery at Ardmore, Déclán travelled among the Déisi, preaching, baptising and building churches. He journeyed further north and preached to King Aongus at Cashel. The king refused baptism because his clan was not on good terms with the Déisi, but he allowed Déclán to work among his people.

The ruined cathedral at Ardmore dates from the ninth century. Two ogham-inscribed grave markers are preserved in its chancel, one of which was described in Chapter 2. By the twelfth century when Déclán's *Life* came to be written, little was known about his work, and the adventures recounted in his biography may have little basis in fact. However, there were traditions about Déclán's love of solitude, and his choice of a 'desert' or place of retreat on the headland 2,600ft beyond the monastery. Here was his hermitage, in a sheltered spot beside a spring.

In old age, he was said to have moved out of the monastic 'city' in order to retire to his Desert. The *Life* relates:

> He lived at that time in a narrow place close to the sea, where a shining stream flows down from the hills above. It is surrounded by trees and bushes, and is called Déclán's Desert. From there, the [monastic] city is about a mile distant, and Déclán went there to avoid noise, so that he could pray and fast there.[5]

Holy well, Déclán's Desert, Ardmore, Waterford.

Déclán's Desert is still a peaceful place surrounded by bushes and trees. In the early morning one can look out across the sparkling sea and watch fishermen in the bay, far below. There are remains of a large ruined church: its east end dates from the fourteenth century, but its west end (*colour plate 2*) is earlier. Beyond the ruined church is Déclán's holy well. Two small doorways lead down to the spring, where it is possible to bathe. The well-house is capped with two late medieval crosses, each bearing a figure of Christ. The well was restored in 1798 and again in 1951. It is visited by countless people, particularly during the week nearest to Déclán's feast day, 24 July. Up to the late 1940s, pilgrims came to spend all night in a prayer vigil at the well.

An account from around 1840 describes the scene on Déclán's feast day:

> The crowd then formed a long line winding up the narrow path that leads along the mountain's brow to St Déclán's chapel … The scenery was beautiful as we looked over the precipitous cliffs across the bay of Ardmore. On the brink stands the remnant of a chapel, said to be the first built in Ireland. On entering the gate, on your right hand is the well St Déclán blessed. Then they knelt down and said their prayers … At twenty different periods, I counted the people as they passed. They averaged fifty-five a minute, which gives a total of twelve or fifteen thousand persons.[6]

Déclán is still one of Ireland's most popular local saints, and his name is commonly given to boys.

The *Life of Déclán* relates that when he sensed death approaching, he returned from his hermitage to the community, to die among his brother monks. We read:

> When Déclán realised that his last days were at hand, he called for Mac Liag from the eastern Déisi, in order to receive the last sacraments from him. He foreknew the day of his death, and asked to be brought back to his own [monastic] city … He was carried back to his city; Mac Liag gave him the last sacraments. He blessed all his people, and when he died, he was buried with honour in the tomb which he had already chosen.[7]

Remains at Ardmore

The chapel of Déclán's Grave is the oldest building of the monastery, although it was restored in the eighteenth century. It is a small rectangular building on eighth-century foundations, built into the hillside on the edge of the site, where the land slopes down to the sea. Large stone blocks form the lower courses of its walls; its projecting pillars, or *antae*, would have supported the roof timbers. Generations of Christians have scooped out earth from Déclán's grave inside the chapel, as it is believed to protect from disease.[8]

*Chapel of Déclán's Grave,
Ardmore, Waterford.*

*Round tower, Ardmore,
Waterford.*

The round tower and the ruined west end of the cathedral at Ardmore date from the twelfth century. A number of fine but badly weathered Romanesque reliefs have been reassembled and set into the cathedral's west wall; they depict Adam and Eve, the adoration of the infant Christ by the three wise men, and other scenes. The round tower was one of the latest to be built in Ireland. Beautifully proportioned, it rises to a height of 95ft; its four tapering storeys are separated by projecting string courses, each resembling a rope. The round-arched doorway is 12ft above ground level. An unusual feature of the tower is that inside are projecting stones carved with grotesque heads.

Towers served as lookout posts and landmarks, guides for sailors and travellers on land. Books, chalices and shrines could be safely stored here, and monks could take refuge in the tower. This one is so strong that it withstood an attack with cannon fire when it was held by the Confederates in 1642, at a time when the native Catholic population struggled against their English Protestant overlords, and Oliver Cromwell ruthlessly repressed the Irish Rebellion. The elegant tower now dominates a peaceful landscape once more.

Ciarán of Saighir

Ciarán is another of the early Munster saints whose chief monastery can still be visited. He lived in the second half of the fifth century, and perhaps died around 530. He is described in two Latin *Lives* and two Irish *Lives*. The second Irish *Life* is the latest, dating from after the Reformation, but it is thought to draw on the oldest traditions. Ciarán's death is also recorded in the *Martyrology of Óengus*, and he is mentioned in medieval Irish genealogies.

He was born in west Cork near Cape Clear, at the southernmost tip of Ireland; a ruined church and well are dedicated to Ciarán on Clear Island. He lived a century before his namesake, Ciarán of Clonmacnoise. According to his *Lives*, as a young man he sailed to mainland Europe, where he was baptised and ordained a priest; he studied at St Martin's monastery in Tours. He returned to his native Ossory, and settled at Saighir, near the Slieve Bloom mountains, first as a hermit and later as abbot of a large monastery. His mother, Liadain, is said to have gone to Saighir with a group of women, to serve God and the monks. Saighir is now the small settlement of Seirkieran, 7 miles north of Roscrea and 40 miles north-east of Limerick; it may have been a pre-Christian site. The monastery is a mile south of Clareen on R421; it is set in rolling hills, with panoramic views in several directions.

A wild boar

His *Life* relates how Ciarán tamed a fierce but frightened wild boar that helped him to collect materials with which to build a church. The author adds: 'This boar was the first disciple, as it were a monk of St Ciarán, in that place'.[9]

A wild boar quite often features in the story of a Celtic monk's chief foundation. Swineherds worked on the edge of settlements, where their pigs could
forage in the forest or in the wilderness, where a monk could find a 'desert
place', in order to seek God.

When a monk searched for the place where he would live and die, which
would become the place of his resurrection, the appearance of a wild boar
came to symbolise God's approval of the site. Readers familiar with the classics
would remember that in Virgil's *Aeneid* a huge white sow showed Ascanius
where to found the great city of Alba Longa, the precursor of Rome.[10] The
boar was also an ancient Celtic symbol of power and authority, and was portrayed on regalia, cauldrons and rock carvings.

Swine appear in a surprising number of saints' *Lives*: six from Ireland (Ciarán
of Saighir, Rúadán, Mochoemóc, Fínán, Fíacc and Finnian of Clonard), four
from Wales (Cadog, Brynach, Dyfrig and Illtud), two from Brittany (Paul
Aurélien and Malo), one from Scotland (Kentigern) and one from Somerset
(Cyngar). The earliest of these is the late eleventh-century *Life of St Cadog* by
Lifris of Llancarfan, in south Wales. In the Irish *Tripartite Life of Patrick*, a pig
digs up gold, with which Patrick pays his ransom. The same source comments
that it would have been more fitting had the young Patrick tended sheep
instead of swine. The earliest vernacular *Life of Brigit*, dating from the ninth
century, describes a miracle concerning pigs in Brigit's care, although the Latin
Life by Cogitosus, which predates it, replaces pigs with sheep.[11]

The pig foundation tales belong to pseudo-history. Typically, a saint who
has been granted a tract of land looks for the best site on which to build a
church; an angel appears in a vision and explains that a pig will show him
the site. Next day, the saint sees the pig, which marks the spot; in the *Life
of St Cadog*, an old bristly white boar leaps out and lands in three separate
places to indicate where a chapel, dormitory and refectory should be built.
Ciarán's wild boar does not follow this typical pattern, but it nevertheless
helps to build the church.

The Easter fire

Ciarán's *Life* also relates how he decreed that the fire in his monastery must
not go out. When it was allowed to do so, and the monks could no longer cook
or warm themselves, Ciarán prayed and the fire lit itself again. The communal
hearth was a central feature of ancient rural communities, and was held to be
holy. In monasteries, the fire lit on Easter night might be kept alive throughout
the following year. It was, of course, difficult to light a fire in a damp climate,
in an age before matches and cigarette lighters.

In a number of saints' *Lives*, fire is rekindled at their prayers, to demonstrate
God's power. Christian readers would recall that the great prophet Elijah kin-
dled fire through his prayer, after the prophets of Baal failed to do so (1 Kgs. 18.
20-40). Fire was symbolic of God's powerful presence: as we saw in Chapter 2,

Patrick's biographer, Muirchú describes how Patrick lit the Easter fire on Slane, in order to celebrate Christ's resurrection, and thereby incurred the wrath of the king of Tara. There is an echo of Elijah's contest with the prophets of Baal when the magi tell the king of Tara:

> This fire, which we see lit this night before the fire of your own house, must be quenched this night. Indeed, if it is not put out tonight, it will never be extinguished! You should know that it will keep rising up and will supplant all the fires of our own religion.[12]

The importance of tending the monastery fire also features in the *Lives* of Brigit, as we saw in the previous chapter; in her case, the nuns ensured that its flames were never extinguished.

Ciarán's monastery

Ciarán's monastery became the seat of the bishops of Ossory, and the burial place of its kings. It was plundered many times, and later became an Augustinian priory. The walled monastic compound covers ten acres. There are a few remains of the Celtic monastery: the stump of a round tower, an early grave slab and the base of a high cross. The water which collects in its socket is believed to cure warts.[13]

Ciarán is a much-loved saint and on his feast day, 5 March, pilgrims flock to Seirkieran. South of the monastery, beside the R421, a signed track leads to Ciarán's well pool. Nearby is Ciarán's Bush: an ancient hawthorn tree to which clouties are tied, as prayers for healing. The aged bush looks strangely out of place on its grassy island, with cars driving past on either side.

Remains of round tower, Seirkieran, Offaly.

Base of high cross, Seirkieran, Offaly.

Kilkieran

There was a monastery dedicated to Ciarán of Saighir at the village of Kilkieran, 5 miles north of Carrick-on-Suir. Its church was on the site where a large later tomb now stands; it was probably surrounded by monks' wooden huts. There are three high crosses at the site: one is unique in design, with its tall thin shaft and stumpy arms; these may have had wooden extensions. The other two crosses are highly elaborate. The ninth-century west cross is particularly fine. On the east side of its base are eight horsemen; the other three sides are decorated with interlacing and geometric patterns. Further down the hill are the remains of what may have been a second early church, close to a pre-Christian standing stone. Nearby is Ciarán's holy well. A boulder with a cavity containing water is known as St Ciarán's Font; its water is believed to cure headaches.[14]

There is another early monastic site dedicated to Ciarán of Saighir at Grangefertagh, between Cullahill and Johnstown, also in Kilkenny. It is close to a crossing point on the River Goul, and is visible from a great distance because of its well-preserved round tower which has eight floors and is 108ft high. The *Annals of the Four Masters* record that the site was raided by Vikings in 861; apart from its round tower, nothing remains from early times.

West cross, Kilkieran, Kilkenny.

Ciarán's holy well, Kilkieran, Kilkenny.

6

VICTIMS OF PLAGUE

P lague was a serious threat to the survival of ancient peoples. Writing in the sixth century BC, the prophet Ezekiel describes the 'four dreadful scourges' of the sword, famine, wild beasts and plague (Ezk. 14. 21), and at the end of the New Testament, the Book of Revelation, written around AD 95, elaborates the theme by describing four deadly riders, mounted on different coloured horses. The fourth horse is 'deathly pale, and its rider was called Plague, and Hades followed at its heels' (Rev. 6. 8).

It was considered very important that Columba and Adomnán could preserve people from plague by their prayer. A plague infecting cattle was in some ways worse than human plague, for it destroyed the basis of the entire economy, depriving people of meat and milk. The litanies of St Mark's day that have survived in 'beating the bounds' were processions round the fields with the relics of saints, to keep the plague away from cattle.[1]

The Yellow Plague

Plague struck Ireland in the 540s; it was named the Yellow Plague (the *Buidhe Connail*), and it spread rapidly in communities where men lived in close proximity to one another. It killed Finnian of Clonard and young Ciarán of Clonmacnoise, among other monastic founders, and peoples' extensive knowledge of herbs and healing were powerless against it.

The Yellow Plague was experienced as a global disaster, which destroyed the fabric of society. Christians are likely to have understood it as punishment for their sins, rather like the expulsion of Adam and Eve from Paradise, after eating the forbidden fruit. Just as Adam and Eve were now condemned to till the soil by the sweat of their brow (Gen. 3. 1-19), people had to precariously begin a new life in difficult circumstances, with a small remnant of their family or religious community.

Perhaps monks who went through this experience saw the plague as a boundary line between themselves and the Age of the Saints. Maybe they looked back to the time when Finnian was abbot of the great monastery of Clonard with its hundreds of monks. His famed followers, the 'Twelve Apostles of Ireland', had gone to God, and now was the post-apostolic period, in which people continued as best they could, at one remove from the sources of monastic holiness.

Plague strikes again

In 664 a total eclipse of the sun on 3 May was dreaded as a portent of evil to come. It was followed by an outbreak of plague which may have been the same as the Yellow Plague a century earlier, or may possibly have been small-pox.[2] It held on tenaciously for twenty years or more.

The *Annals of the Four Masters* records sadly:

> 664. A great mortality prevailed in Ireland this year, which was called the *Buidhe Connail*, and the following number of the saints of Ireland died of it: St Féichín, abbot of Fore on 14 February; St Ronan, son of Bearach; St Aileran the Wise; St Cronan, son of Silne; St Mánchan, of Liath; St Ultán, ... Abbot of Clonard; Colmán, ... Abbot of Clonmacnoise; and Cummine, Abbot of Clonmacnoise ... There died very many ecclesiastics and laymen in Ireland of this mortality besides these.
>
> 665. Yellow Plague outbreak at Fore Abbey.
>
> 666. A great plague raged this year, of which died four abbots ...[3]

Bede tells us that the same plague ravaged Northumbria; he describes how Bishop Cedd died at Lastingham. When his people at Bradwell-on-Sea in Essex heard the news, thirty of them travelled northwards to pay their respects: all but one, a boy, died of the plague like Cedd.[4]

Finnian of Clonard

Finnian (d. *c.* 549) was one of the most significant monastic founders who succumbed to the Yellow Plague; he was considered to be the father of Irish monasticism. The tenth-century *Life of Finnian*, preserved in the *Book of Lismore*, relates that he was born and educated in Carlow in south-east Ireland, where he made several foundations. It recounts that he then travelled to south Wales, where he spent time in the great Welsh monasteries.

He returned to Ireland and established two more communities before settling at Clonard in Meath.

The *Life* presents Finnian as a very influential leader: 3000 monks studied at Clonard, and so great was Finnian's reputation that he was nicknamed 'Teacher of the saints of Ireland'. When monks left Clonard, they took with them a gospel book, a crosier or a reliquary, as they set out to establish their own communities. As we have seen, twelve leading Irish monks were considered to be Finnian's disciples, and were known as 'The Twelve Apostles of Ireland'; among them were Ciarán of Clonmacnoise, Kevin of Glendalough, Brendan and Columba. Several of these 'apostles' had died before Finnian's lifetime, or had not yet been born, but the list indicates Clonard's considerable influence.

Clonard

Finnian chose a central location for his chief monastery, only 30 miles from the east coast, within easy reach of mainland Britain and Europe. The settlement was in fertile farmland beside the River Boyne; cows grazing the site today are a reminder that the rich pasture could support a large community. There have been sample excavations at the extensive monastic site, but few remains have been uncovered. Down a signed grassy track, a modern church stands within an ancient graveyard. Set in the ground near the church porch is a large rectangular stone basin or *lavabo* which originally contained water for washing;

Early lavabo, *Clonard churchyard, Meath.*

Finnian depicted on the font in Clonard church, Meath.

it may date from early times. Its brackish water was said to cause death to animals but to cure warts.

Another artefact which has survived is a tiny elaborate bucket, bound with a bronze hoop; its handle clasps are decorated with fine carving and precious stones. The bucket was perhaps used to contain holy water.[5] Finnian's relics were enshrined at Clonard until the monastery was destroyed in 887; it was rebuilt in the twelfth century, and its monks adopted the Augustinian rule. A magnificent fifteenth-century font of grey marble limestone survives from the abbey. It can be seen in the apse behind the high altar in the modern Catholic church beside the busy N6 in Clonard village. Lively scenes are carved on its panels: Joseph leads a donkey by its halter as the Holy Family flees into Egypt, and a smiling Bishop Finnian raises his hand in blessing, while an angel beside him holds a gospel book.

Finnian's *Penitential*

The *Penitential of Finnian* was probably written at Clonard in the late sixth century. This is a manual of punishments for crimes, based partly on Irish and Welsh sources, and also on the writings of Jerome and Cassian; much of it, however, is original. It is the oldest of the Irish Penitentials, which made an important contribution to the Church's understanding of pastoral care. They were written to regulate attitudes and conduct in monasteries, and also for lay people. In the Penitentials, sin is considered a disease, and penance a medicine; the abbot is the monk's healer or physician. Sin is also regarded as an offence, and penance a judgement, with the abbot a discerning judge.

The Penitentials were not abstract treatises, but practical commentaries based on experience. Their underlying theology is positive: there is no sin which is outside the mercy of God. They embody gospel attitudes: 'What goes into the mouth does not make a man unclean; it is what comes out of the mouth that makes him unclean' (Mt. 15. 11). The Penitentials contain scripture-based remedies for sin; their legacy was long lasting and they were pastorally effective. They shifted the emphasis from crime to therapy, from recovering lost purity to becoming whole.

Irish monks took the *Penitential of Finnian* and subsequent examples to Europe; they perhaps form insular Christianity's most important bequest to mainland Europe. The earliest copies of Finnian's *Penitential* are found in three ninth-century manuscripts in St Gall and Paris. The work begins gently:

> In the name of the Father and of the Son and of the Holy Ghost.
> 1. If anyone has sinned in the thoughts of his heart and immediately repents, he shall beat his breast and seek pardon from God and make satisfaction, that he may be whole.[6]

It gradually addresses more serious faults: quarrelling, lust, practising magic and murder, prescribing suitable penances for specific situations. Finnian believed that every sin, however serious, could be atoned for: 'There is no crime which cannot be expiated through penance, as long as we are in this body'.

The Letter from Gildas to Finnian

Finnian consulted the renowned theologian, Gildas, about issues such as abstinence from food and monks who arrived from other monasteries. A *Pastoral Letter* written by Gildas in response to Finnian survives. The *Letter* is elegant and clear:

> ... Abstinence from bodily food is useless without charity ... They eat bread by the measure – but boast about it beyond measure; they use water – but at the same time drink the cup of hatred; they enjoy dry fare – and at the same time enjoy backbiting. They keep their vigils long, while criticising others plunged in sleep .... They prefer fasting to charity, vigils to justice, their own contrivances to concord, the cell to the church, severity to humility, man to God.[7]

The letter became well known in monastic circles: writing in about 600, fifty years after Finnian's death, the missionary Columbanus praised the *Pastoral Letter* for its wisdom, in a letter of his own to Pope Gregory the Great. In it, he reminded the pope that Gildas wrote 'a most judicious reply' to 'the eminent Finnian'.[8]

Finnian and Columba

Adomnán, the ninth abbot of Iona, informs us that, as a young man Columba was a disciple of 'Finnio'. In his *Life of Columba*, Adomnán describes a meeting between the elderly Finnio and young Columba. He relates:

> At another time, the holy man [Columba] went to the venerable Bishop Finnio, his teacher, as a young man to an old. When Saint Finnio saw him approaching him, he saw besides an angel of the Lord accompanying his journey, and, as we are told on reliable authority, he informed some brothers who were standing by, saying, 'Behold, see now the holy Columba coming here, who has proved worthy to have an angel of heaven to share his travel'.[9]

Adomnán here conveys that his patron Columba is perhaps more holy than the venerable Finnian.

British influence on Irish monasteries

It is now thought likely that Finnian of Movilla, named after a monastery which he established in County Down, may be the same person as Finnian of Clonard. It was claimed that Finnian of Movilla was educated at Ninian's monastery of Whithorn, in Galloway; however, it may be that Finnian founded Whithorn: the name Ninian is attested in only a limited form, and Bede's early date for Ninian is questionable.[10]

It was not until the twelfth century that Aelred of Rievaulx claimed that Ninian was a contemporary of Martin of Tours; no material was found at Whithorn dating earlier than the sixth century. The size of the monastic settlement suggests a British saint, Finnian, who was also active in Ireland. There is a Chapel Finnian within walking distance of the monastery, and a Kirfinny Farm nearby.[11]

It is also likely that monasticism reached Ireland through Wales at the end of the fifth and the beginning of the sixth century. Ireland had considerable contact with Roman Wales and there is some evidence of flourishing monasteries in south Wales, particularly that of Illtud, who is thought to have been active around 520, at Llanilltud Fawr. Cadog of Llancarfan and Gildas are said to have been associated with Illtud. In the following generation, written sources record the presence of British monks among the followers of Columba and Columbanus.[12]

Ciarán of Clonmacnoise

It must have been particularly tragic when young monks died of plague. Ciarán of Clonmacnoise was a man of great promise who died young. *Lives* of the saint written centuries later describe him as the son of an Ulsterman who had settled in Connaght. Their authors record that, unlike many Irish abbots, Ciarán was not of noble birth. They indicate that he was a holy man by stating that, like Jesus, Ciarán was a carpenter's son who died in 549 at the age of thirty-three. He was said to have studied under Finnian of Clonard, with Enda in the Aran Islands and later still with Senan on Scattery Island.

A story set in Ciarán's student days at Clonard reflects the later importance of his own monastery: while Ciarán was reading his copy of Matthew's Gospel, a poorer student asked to borrow the book. Ciarán had studied only the first half, but lent it to him at once. Next day in class, Ciarán could answer questions only on the first half of the text, and his companions joked about 'Ciarán half-Matthew'. Abbot Finnian commented, 'Not Ciarán half-Matthew but Ciarán half-Ireland, for he will have half of Ireland and ourselves the other half'.

Clonmacnoise

Ciarán founded a community on an island in Lough Ree, further north on the Shannon, before settling at Clonmacnoise, whose name means 'water mead-ows of the sons of Nós'. Ciarán selected a key point on the broad river, near the Athlone ford and on the sandy esker ridge that forms the great east-west road across central Ireland. Today, passing boats are a reminder that the Shannon, Ireland's longest river, was a major route north and south, so Clonmacnoise was situated at the main crossroads of Ireland. The water meadows flood annually and provide rich pasture that could support a large community. Annals compiled at Clonmacnoise describe its foundation by Ciarán in the 540s, on land given to him by Diarmaid Mac Cerbhaill of the royal house of Uí Néill. Diarmaid helped to build the first wooden church with his own hands, and soon afterwards became high king. Within a year, Ciarán was dead.

Early evidence

Little survives from Ciarán's monastery. Pieces of sixth-century pottery have been found, and in 1990 an ogham-inscribed gravestone was discovered, perhaps dating from the fifth or sixth century. It is the first to have been found in this region of Ireland; later it was used for sharpening iron tools. It lay beneath the new graveyard, at the eastern end of the monastic site. Further excavation uncovered a roadway, traces of houses, corn-drying kilns and a boat slip. At the opposite end of the site, beyond the round tower, under-water excavation carried out in 1994–98 uncovered the remains of a wooden bridge across the Shannon. Tree-ring dating of its oak timbers suggests that it was built in about 804.[13]

Teampaill Ciarán, *Clonmacnoise, Offaly.*

Near the centre of the compound is the smallest of the churches, *Teampaill Ciarán*. According to tradition, Ciarán was buried here, and pilgrims used to take home soil from the grave to heal their sick. A relic known as St Ciarán's Hand was kept here until 1684, when the chapel was still roofed. The early tenth-century building has putlog holes in its walls: these held timbers to which scaffolding was tied during the chapel's construction. Its walls are no longer vertical, since so many burials around the founder's tomb have caused the earth to shift.

High crosses

In the north-west corner of the monastic compound is a replica of one of Ireland's finest high crosses, referred to in the annals as 'the Cross of the Scriptures' (*colour plate 8*). Its shaft and head were carved from a single piece of sandstone, and an inscription round its base asks prayers for King Flann and for Abbot Colmán who made it. Colmán was abbot from about 904 to 926, and erected the largest of the churches on the site. Behind the cross stands a ruined round tower; annalists record its completion in 1124. However, storms caused damage in the following decades: in 1135 the top of the tower was struck off by lightning. In 1149 St Ciarán's yew tree was also felled by lightning, and 113 sheep sheltering beneath it were killed.

The South Cross was carved in the ninth century; a damaged inscription on its base suggests that it was commissioned by the father of King Flann, who is mentioned on the Cross of the Scriptures. Both these sandstone crosses were probably quarried in Clare, transported up the Shannon, and carved here in the monastic workshops. Much of the South Cross is covered with abstract ornament, in the form of interlacing and fretwork, spirals and bosses. This style of decoration appears to derive from earlier metal-encased wooden crosses. The elaborate bosses echo the shapes and patterns found on metalwork and jewellery of the period.[14]

Columba visits Clonmacnoise

Despite Ciarán's early death, Clonmacnoise grew rapidly in importance. Adomnán wrote in his *Life of Columba* (*c.* 690) that when Alither was abbot of Clonmacnoise, Columba paid him a visit. He relates:

> When they heard of [Columba's] approach, everyone in the fields near the monastery came from all directions. Together with those inside the monastery, they most eagerly accompanied their abbot, Alither. They passed beyond the enclosure wall of the property and with one accord they went to meet St Columba, as if he were an angel of the Lord.[15]

Adomnán hints here that Iona was rather more important than Clonmacnoise.

By the seventh century, Clonmacnoise had a large non-monastic popula-tion, and had acquired many dependent churches, which led to disputes over property. In about 700, Tírechán, the biographer of Patrick, complained that the community of Clonmacnoise forcibly held many churches that had been founded by Patrick. In spite of their rapturous welcome of Columba, a further dispute arose between the monks of Clonmacnoise and those of Columba's foundation at Durrow, 35 miles south-east. Monks from the two communities fought each other in 764, and 200 men from Durrow were killed.[16]

Life at the monastery

There was intensive settlement around the monastery, with circular houses where artisans lived with their families: metalworkers in iron and bronze, gold and silver, and craftsmen skilled in antler working or comb-making. There were also stone masons who, besides carving crosses, produced some 700 grave markers over a period of four hundred years. A piece of scratched bone that was used by an apprentice to practise plaitwork patterns still survives: his attempts were rather unskilled.

Since Ciarán was not of noble birth and his family was not native to the area, he left no dynasty from which abbots might be chosen. His family was not represented among later abbots, and the monastery remained independ-ent of other clans. Chroniclers in the community kept records of significant

events from at least the eighth century, and it is possible to com-pile an almost complete list of abbots from Ciarán's time until the twelfth century. The settlement's churches were burnt down more than thirty times during this period by accident, by Irish kings and by Viking raiders.

Monks in the scriptorium must have illuminated fine gospel books, but none have survived. However, the ornate metalwork shrine of the *Stowe Missal* (c. 1030) bears an inscription stating that it was crafted by a monk of Clonmacnoise. Some secular texts written by the monks have been

Teampaill Finghin, *Clonmacnoise, Offaly.*

The Nuns' Church, Clonmacnoise, Offaly.

preserved, including the *Book of the Dun Cow*, which contains the earliest known version of the *Cattle Raid of Cooley* (*Táin Bó Cúailnge*), in a manuscript dating from around 1100.

The annals record that in 1013 the great oak of Finghin's churchyard was blown down in a storm. *Teampaill Finghin* is on the northern boundary of the enclosure, exposed to winds whipping across the meadowland from the Shannon below. The ruined stone church on the site has a unique belfry which also served as a round tower. With such frequent raids, the monks may have felt the need for this second tower into which they could hurry for protection. The belfry is set at the junction of the chancel and the nave; its conical cap is well preserved.

One of the main approach roads to the monastery from the east leads past the Nuns' Church. It continues through the graveyard, where its large stone slabs have been named the Pilgrims' Way. On a gravel ridge to the right of the road, halfway to the Nuns' Church, a small platform of stones appears to be the Cairn of the Three Crosses which monks mention in the annals. In summer the grass here is bright with purple orchids and other flowers. In 1026 a chronicler describes the construction of a causeway from the piglets' yard to the Cross of Congal. We learn other details: in 1104, the cathedral roof was covered with wooden slates. A collection of treasures was stolen from the high altar in 1129 by a Scandinavian plunderer. He was tracked down in Limerick the following year and hanged by the king of Munster, and the monks recovered their treasures.

The Nuns' Church

The Nuns' Church and its cemetery is 1,640ft east of the main site, within its own enclosure. According to the chronicles, in the cemetery was a stone church which was burnt down in 1082; its remains are incorporated into an adjoining field wall. The annals relate that the present church was completed in 1167 by Dearbhforgaill, wife of the king of Breifne. The overking of Leinster abducted her during a raid, and apparently she was not unwilling to be captured.

The monastic chronicler records with disapproval how the king of Leinster 'kept her for a long time to satisfy his insatiable, carnal and adulterous lust', before returning her the following year. Her husband later drove the king of Leinster into exile, but the overking sought help from Henry II of England, and thus the Anglo-Norman invasion began. In 1186, at the mature age of seventy-eight, Queen Dearbhforgaill retired to the Cistercian abbey of Mellifont, where she died seven years later.[17]

Féchín of Fore

Féchín was a holy man from Sligo who fell victim to the second devastating outbreak of plague, over a century after the first, in about 665. He is mentioned in Irish annals, martyrologies, genealogies and hagiographical works. There are two surviving *Lives of Féchín*, one in Latin and the other in Irish. The Latin *Life* was written around 1400, its chief source appearing to be a *Life* originating in Féchín's monastery on Omey Island. The Irish *Life* was written by Nicol Óg, son of the abbot of Cong, in 1328. The first part of Óg's *Life* is chiefly concerned with Féchín's position as negotiator between the Luigne of Connacht, to whom he supposedly belonged, and the more powerful Muigne of Meath, in whose territory Fore Abbey was founded. The second part is more concerned with Leinster and the payment of tribute.

Féchín's nicknames

Féchín is said to have been born in Bile (probably Billa), 6 miles south-south-west of Sligo. His two *Lives* relate that Féchín studied under St Nath Í of Achonry, and later moved to Clonmacnoise. A note added to the *Martyrology of Óengus* explains that his name means Little Raven (*mo fiachan*), because when his mother saw how young Féchín gnawed on a bone, she exclaimed 'My Little Raven!'.

The same note also names him *Moéca*, which is explained as meaning 'backslider', for when Féchín received too little for herding the oxen at Ciarán's monastery of Clonmacnoise, he left in anger. He was asked to return, changed his mind, and crept back. This may be an allusion to the parable of Jesus in which one son agreed to work in his father's vineyard, but changed his mind and did not go, while the other son refused, but later changed his mind and went to work after all (Mt. 21. 28-31). The second son is praised for changing his mind because he thought better of his behaviour and returned, despite the loss of face involved. Féchín proved himself a good monk by risking loss of face and the shame incurred, by repenting of his anger.

Féchín's monasteries

Féchín's first foundations are said to have been those on the islands of Omey and Ardoilén, both off the Galway coast. His chief monastery was at Fore, in Westmeath. Places connected with Féchín's cult include, among others, Cong (Mayo), Inis Meáin (Aran Islands, Galway), Ballysadare (3 miles from his birthplace in Sligo), and Abbey (*Mhainistir*, in Galway). There are monastic ruins at most of Féchín's foundations, a few dating from his lifetime. Holy wells are dedicated to him throughout Ireland, especially in the west. His cult was taken by his followers to Scotland, where the monastery of St Vigeans at Arbroath near the Fife coast is named after him. An impressive collection of Pictish inscribed stones survives at the monastery.

Fore

Féchín's first foundation was at Fore, 20 miles west of Navan. It is an interesting site: in the tenth century a simple rectangular church was built on the hillside here. Its west doorway can be seen in the photograph: on its giant lintel is a carved cross within a circular design. A small graveyard surrounds the church, which was burnt at least twelve times between 771 and 1169.

The monastery was a bishopric until the twelfth century, when the Normans built a large Benedictine abbey in the valley below, and life probably ended at Féchín's foundation. Between the two sites, a ruined mill is said to be on the site of one built by Féchín. It is fed by underground streams from Lough Lene, a mile away, on the far side of the mountain. The rivulets emerge from the hillside and flow into a triangular millpond before continuing through the ruined mill.

Between the mill and the Benedictine abbey, beneath an ancient ash tree, is Féchín's holy well. It is a triangular structure, its walls formed by three great stone slabs; it is named *Doaghféighín*, or Féchín's Vat. It is now dry, but formerly contained water in which Féchín was said to have knelt in prayer. Delicate children were immersed in the water to be cured through Féchín's intercession.[18] Gnarled roots of the ash tree are now entwined with the stones of Féchín's Vat. Clouties are tied to the tree, as mute prayers for healing.

Entrance to Féchín's church, Fore, Westmeath.

Cong

Féchín founded a monastery at Cong, from which little survives except a multiple bullaun stone, *Leach na bPoll*, a large triangular flagstone with five basin-like hollows in it, now on private land. This may have been used by early monks requiring a mortar and pestle in the smelting process. Cong is at the northern end of Lough Corrib; its name derives from the Gaelic word *Conga* ('a narrow neck of land'): this describes the isthmus between Lough Corrib and Lough Mask on which the settlement is built.

Saints Fursa, Cuanga and Annin are early monks who lived around Lough Corrib. The lough enters the ocean at Galway city, via the Corrib River; it is rich in fish, and so could well sustain a large monastery with food. It is home to a variety of freshwater fish: brown trout, pike, perch and roach. Salmon swim from Nova Scotia up the Corrib River into the lough, and eels arrive from the Sargasso Sea in the North Atlantic Ocean, between the West Indies and the Azores.

The magnificent Cross of Cong was carved at the monastery in about 1123; it is a processional cross made of oak decorated with metal filigree, designed to enclose a relic of the cross of Christ at its centre. It is now in the National Museum, Dublin. At about the time that the cross was made, the Celtic monastery was destroyed by fire; the present abbey was built on the same site in 1135 by the last High Kings of Ireland, the O'Connor Kings Turlough, Rory and Cathal.

Several years later, the monks adopted the Augustinian rule. Soon after, in 1203, the Norman knight William de Burgo attacked and destroyed the town, and again the monastery had to be rebuilt. The sculpture in the abbey is some of the finest in Ireland, and suggests links with western France. The abbey was suppressed in 1542 by King Henry VIII; the modern village of Cong now covers much of the monastic site.

An ancient yew tree walk leads from the monastery to the Monks' Fishing House (*colour plate 9*). Fish was a staple diet, and this small fifteenth- or sixteenth-century

Chapter house doorway, Cong, Mayo.

building made the monks' task of catching fish easier. It is built on a platform of stones over a small arch which allows water from the river to flow underneath the floor. A trapdoor in the floor may have been used for a net, and monks could sit by the small fireplace in cold weather, waiting for their catch.[19]

Féchín's 'great church', Ballysadare

The smaller sites associated with Féchín are also interesting. One of these is near his birthplace, 4 miles south-west of Sligo at the head of Ballysadare Bay, where the river enters the sea. The name Ballysadare (*Baile Easa Dara*) means 'homestead of the waterfall of the oak', so it is possible that the settlement was established beside a pre-Christian holy oak tree. The church is known as *Teampaill Mór Féchín* (or Féchín's great church). It is located on the west bank of the Ballysadare River, overlooking the waterfall, and is now largely covered with ivy. Fishing would have been easy in the bay below the monastery.

The oldest feature of the church is the western gable and a section of the adjoining north wall; the church has been rebuilt a number of times. The present structure dates from the thirteenth century, and incorporates twelfth-century stonework. A Romanesque doorway has been inserted into the south wall; it is decorated with carved heads. A tympanum, or decorated space above the entrance arch, may have adorned what is now a plain surface.

At its west end, St Féchín's church was once divided into an upper and a lower level: there is a row of holes for joists in the south wall. A number of fragments of sculpture from the church are now in the National Museum, Dublin, including a portion of its Romanesque font, deco-rated with palm fronds and other patterns. Lying 820ft to the west is a fifteenth-century Augustinian church, now almost buried beneath the debris from a quarry.[20]

Romanesque doorway, Féchín's 'great church', Ballysadare, Sligo.

Abbey

The Irish name of this village in Galway, *Mhainistir*, tells us that this was a monastic site. Abbey's various names in early records, Kilnahan, Kinalekin and Kynnaleighen, are transliterations of the Gaelic *Cinéal Féichín*, meaning 'the tribe of Féchín'. In about 1253, John de Cogan invited Carthusian monks to settle here; they built Kilnahan Abbey around 1268. As the only Carthusian abbey in Ireland, it did not flourish, and the building was taken over by the Knights Hospitallers. Later, in about 1371, it became a Franciscan friary. The Franciscans remained here after the Reformation, until the end of the eighteenth century.

There are *turas* in the abbey grounds, where pilgrims pray at specific locations (literally 'make a tour'); one of the *turas* is Ladywell, which is said to cure eyes, toothache and warts. It is a rainwater well, so a cure can be sought only after heavy rain. Local people come to 'make the pattern', or complete the prayers, from 15 August, the feast of the Assumption, to 8 September, Our Lady's birthday.[21] Abbey is on R353 in County Galway, 8 miles west of Portumna and 12 miles south-east of Loughrea. St Féchín's well is a mile away, in a field on the hillside above Abbey (*colour plate 10*). It healed eye diseases; an old thorn tree grows over it. In order to find it, ask for the memorial park, which is to the right of the field.

The well pool, Kilnahan Friary, Abbey, Galway.

Féchín's death

According to the *Annals of the Four Masters*, Féchín died in 664/5 during the plague. A curious story about his death is found in the Latin *Life* of St Gerald of Mayo and in the notes to the hymn *Sén Dé*, by Colmán moccu Clúasaig in the eleventh-century *Liber Hymnorum*.[22] It relates that the joint high kings Diarmait Ruanaid and Blathmac asked Féchín and various other monks to fast in order to ask God to inflict a plague on the lower classes of society, in order to decrease their number, since the land was becoming overpopulated. Féchín was one of those who answered the kings' request and perished, while Gerald remained aloof and survived. We are left to decide whether this was a regrettable lack of compassion on Féchín's part, or whether followers of St Gerald devised the story to discredit Féchín.

7

BRENDAN THE NAVIGATOR

Brendan (d. *c.* 575) was a monk of Munster origin. His family name, moccu Altai, indicates that he belonged to the Alltraige, a tribe who lived in the region of north Kerry. Brendan was said to have been tutored by Bishop Erc of Kerry, and to have been one of the 'twelve apostles' who followed the leadership of Finnian of Clonard (see Chapter 6). His *Life* was perhaps written before 800, while the earliest surviving copies date from the late twelfth century. Throughout medieval times, Brendan was a patron of sailors, and churches in many coastal settlements are named after him.

Brendan sails to Scotland

Brendan seems to have been one of many monks who chose the ocean as a focus for their monastic exile. His *Life* relates how he sailed to Argyll, on the Scottish west coast: 'Brendan of Clonfert came to a certain island of Britain called Ailech, and there he founded a church, proposing to remain there to the end'.[1] This appears to refer to an islet named *Eileach an Naomh* ('the Holy Rocks'), the southernmost of the Garvellach Isles, where a cluster of monastic cells clings to its cliffs, with a cemetery and remains of other buildings.[2]

The Garvellachs are 5 miles south of the large island of Mull, in the Firth of Lorne. The *Life* describes how Brendan 'prayed alone near the sea on a lofty rock'. This rocky islet is very different from the more fertile islands in the region chosen by Columba for his self-supporting monasteries. Writing in the seventh century, Adomnán says that Brendan visited Columba on the island of Hinba: this is likely to be the large, fertile island of Jura, 5 miles south of the Garvellachs. Adomnán describes four Irish abbots, Congall,

Cainnech, Cormac and Brendan celebrating Sunday Eucharist with Columba in his monastery on Jura.[3]

Ardfert

The two chief sites where Brendan is commemorated on the Irish mainland are Ardfert and Clonfert. The cathedral at Ardfert is in his own tribal territory, 3 miles from the Kerry coast; the discovery of an ogham-inscribed stone and some graves beneath the eleventh-century cathedral indicate that this was an early monastic site. However, since Brendan himself left this region, choosing the life of a *peregrinus*, Ardfert is unlikely to have been linked with Brendan until after his death.

Ardfert means 'height of the graves', and much of north Kerry is visible from the low ridge on which the monastery was built. A stone church on the site was damaged by lightning in 1046; some of its masonry survives in the cathedral's north wall. A round tower was built at this time; it collapsed in 1776, and only its base remains.

In the twelfth century, Ardfert was declared a diocese. Some time after 1130, a fine Romanesque cathedral was built, with an imposing west doorway modelled on Cormac's Chapel at Cashel. The rest of the cathedral was later rebuilt. There are two smaller churches within the monastic enclosure; the earliest, named *Teampaill na Hoe* (or 'church of the Virgin'), was built in the twelfth century. It has a steeply pitched roof and, unusually, columns with carved capitals decorate its outer corners. A second church, *Teampaill na Griffin*, was built beside it in the fifteenth century.

Romanesque doorway, Ardfert Cathedral, Kerry.

Teampaill na Hoe, *Ardfert Cathedral, Kerry.*

Clonfert

Brendan's monastery of Clonfert is 13 miles south-east of Ballinasloe, and 2 miles west of the River Shannon. The larger monastery of Clonmacnoise (see Chapter 6) is not far away on the opposite bank, and rivalry was to develop between the two communities concerning the ownership of property, as we shall see. The name Clonfert means 'water meadow of the graves', and well describes the fertile low-lying site where people brought their dead for burial alongside the monks. Brendan is believed to have founded Clonfert around 558, about twenty years before his death, and is thought to be buried here. It was pillaged by Danes who sailed up the Shannon from Limerick and burned the monastery in 1016, 1164 and 1179.

The present cathedral dates from the end of the twelfth century. It is a simple single-chambered building, with *antae*, or pillars projecting beyond the walls, at each gable, designed to support the roof timbers. The chancel was added in the early thirteenth century, and a beautiful, simple east window was added at this time. A door in the north wall of the chancel leads to a sacristy, in which marks of the wattle roof can be seen in the low plastered ceiling.

Clonfert's magnificent west doorway is perhaps the finest example of twelfth-century Irish Romanesque carving; it was constructed under Bishop Peter O'Moore (1161–71). The door is surmounted by a pediment decorated with carved men's heads, set within a geometric design. Some heads are old

The west doorway, Clonfert, Galway.

and bearded, while others are young and clean-shaven. It recalls the ancient Celtic head-cult, in which the entrance to a chieftain's stronghold might be adorned with the potent heads of ancestors or foes. Carved around the doorway are a variety of animals' heads, suggesting Scandinavian influence.

The first stage of the *Navigatio sancti Brendani abbatis*, or *Voyage of St Brendan the abbot*, one of the most popular stories in medieval times, is set in Clonfert. As if to illustrate the story, a fifteenth-century mermaid is carved on the chancel arch of the cathedral. She lures unwary monks to destruction as she combs her long, sensuous hair, resting a mirror on her naked body.

There was a large monastery at Clonfert throughout medieval times until the Reformation. A State Paper from the reign of Elizabeth I records that before Trinity College, Dublin, was founded, it was proposed to establish the university at Clonfert, since at that time it was known as a seat of learning, and it was in a central location for Irish students. However, the monastery and church were destroyed in 1541, and the monastery was never rebuilt.

The *Penitential of Cummíne*

About a hundred years after Brendan, Cummíne Fota ('the Tall') became bishop of Clonfert. He was a celebrated hymn writer, and in about 650 he compiled the *Penitential of Cummíne*; that of Finnian was described in the previous chapter. Cummíne's is the most comprehensive of the Irish Penitentials. He used Welsh sources and, following the scheme adopted by John Cassian, he grouped and codified sins according to the 'eight capital sins' of gluttony, fornication, envy, anger, dejection, avarice, vainglory and pride.

Cummíne applied Cassian's principle of 'healing through opposites', which derives from Greek medical theory: thus the talkative monk was to be punished with silence, and the sleepy monk by watching in prayer. His approach to erring monks was gentle and compassionate, and he was also concerned for victims of crime:

> He who by a blow in a quarrel renders a man incapacitated or maimed shall meet [the injured man's] medical expenses and shall make good the damages for the deformity and shall do his work until he is healed and do penance for half a year ...[4]

It is typical of Cummíne's compassion that the Penitential ends by exhorting the confessor to weigh up the individual strengths and weaknesses of the sinner and take them into account when imposing a penance on him. Later Irish Penitentials drew on that of Cummíne, and its influence can be seen in the *Rule of St Benedict*. It circulated widely in mainland Europe during the eighth and ninth centuries. Cummíne probably died in the plague of 662.

Annaghdown

Annaghdown is an early site, whose name, *Eanach nDhúin*, means 'the marsh of the fort'. The name probably refers to the marshlands attached to the fort of the local chieftain, which would have been granted as a site for a church. It was said that Brendan established a convent for his sister beside an inlet of Lough Corrib at Annaghdown, and that Brendan died here, before his remains were interred at Clonfert. These statements appear to derive from a later attempt by Clonfert to justify its claim on Annaghdown, whose name does not appear in annals until the twelfth century, by which time it is said to have been granted to St Brendan of Clonfert by King Áed mac Echach of Connacht.[5]

However, Áed's territory was some distance away, in Roscommon, so it may not have been his to grant to Brendan. It seems more likely that the site belonged to Clonmacnoise, on the opposite bank of the Shannon, since the *Comanmniguid Noem nErenn*, composed around 800, refers to 'Ciarán of Annaghdown' (*Ciarán Enaigh nDúin*), claiming the site for the founder of Clonmacnoise. Annaghdown diocese was established in the twelfth century, and survived for some centuries, but the cathedral fought a losing battle throughout medieval times to assert its independence from the archbishopric of Tuam.[6] There are considerable remains of a twelfth-century priory at the site, 330ft to the west; a Romanesque window, possibly taken from the priory, has been inserted into the fifteenth-century cathedral church.

Voyage tales

Brendan's *Navigatio* was probably written after his *Life*, in the mid-ninth century, perhaps at Clonfert. Its style resembles that of an *immram*, or 'rowing story': this was a literary form popular in the seventh and eighth centuries, in which a hero with a few companions, often monks, sails from island to island in the ocean, encounters otherworld wonders, and finally returns home. The Latin voyage tales are partly factual and partly symbolic: monks were actually sailing on voyages, but the stories were also moral tales, describing our journey through life towards heaven.

The stories were heard by both monks and lay people, and were partly satiri-cal: Brendan sails for seven years, in search of the Promised Land, but finally the monastic steward tells him that it is to be found back east, at home. The theme of voyagers travelling to the edge of the world was attractive to medieval listeners; a modern equivalent would perhaps be the *Star Trek* saga. Brendan's *Navigatio* became popular throughout Europe, and was translated into German, Dutch, French and Italian. It may have been preceded by an earlier voyage tale, *Immram Brain*, whose subject was perhaps a pagan deity named Bran, of whom the Irish hero and Bran, the Welsh hero in the *Mabinogion* may be manifestations.

The Voyage of Bran

In the surviving fifteenth-century manuscript of this tale, Bran is in his fort, sitting with other chieftains, behind locked doors. A woman passes by from the otherworld with a blossoming branch, singing. She declaims fifty poems describing places that are part of her realm, including a plain which is both on land and sea, islands where birds sing the canonical hours, and white cliffs. These themes reappear in Brendan's *Navigatio*: a plain which is both land and sea recalls how the waters of the Red Sea receded to allow the Israelite slaves to escape from the Egyptians (Exodus 14), and the white cliffs are likely to represent icebergs. The birds also chant the monastic Office in Brendan's story.

Brendan set out on his voyage from the foot of Brandon Mountain in the Dingle peninsula, where some places are named after Bran, such as a point called *Sron Broin*, meaning Bran's Snout or nuzzle. The relationship between the two texts is complex: it is possible that the two voyage tales influenced each other, with Bran seen as a kind of Old Testament hero. *The Voyage of Bran* perhaps takes something familiar and places it in the past, as a commentary upon the present. Bran is an important figure in early Welsh literature, and may have been part of a wider cosmology.[7]

Brendan's Voyage

The *Navigatio* had a very wide appeal, because people searching for the desert in the ocean were seen as heroic, exciting figures who pushed the boundaries of human existence. According to the story, Brendan was living at Clonfert as abbot of a community of about 3000 brothers, when he was visited by a monk named Barrind. This traveller had visited the island monastery of St Mernóc, near Slieve League in Donegal, more than 150 miles to the north. Barrind described Mernóc's monastery as an ideal community in which monks lived in scattered dwellings, but gathered to celebrate the Eucharist like the monks of the Near Eastern deserts. They ate frugally and kept the great silence each night.

While Barrind was staying with Mernóc, he was told about the Promised Land of the Saints. Barrind had set sail through thick fog and reached the heavenly Jerusalem, full of precious stones, with all its plants in flower and a river flowing across it from east to west. Barrind describes his experience using words taken from chapters 21 and 22 of the Book of Revelation at the end of the New Testament. Barrind added that he had returned home after a year.

1. *Hermits' caves, Wadi Fayran, Sinai.*

2. *Déclán's Desert, Ardmore, Waterford.*

3. *Kevin's Desert, Glendalough, Wicklow.*

4. *High cross, Diarmaid's Desert, Castledermot, Kildare.*

5. Teampaill Breacáin, The Seven Churches, *Inis Mór, Aran Islands.*

6. *St Brigit's church, Iniscealtra, Clare.*

7. *Early stones at St Attracta's well, Kiltura, Sligo.*

8. High cross and round tower, Clonmacnoise, Offaly.

9. *Monks' Fishing House, Cong Abbey, Mayo.*

10. *St Féchín's well, Abbey, Galway.*

11. *Curraghs moored in Brandon Creek, Kerry.*

12. East face of high cross, Drumcliffe, Sligo.

13. *Columba's well, Durrow, Offaly.*

14. *General view, Gleanncholmcille, Donegal.*

15. Decorated cross-pillar on a rocky outcrop, station 2, Gleanncholmcille, Donegal.

16. *Caldragh Cemetery, Boa Island, Lower Lough Erne, Fermanagh.*

17. *Twelfth-century church, White Island, Lower Lough Erne, Fermanagh.*

18. *Round tower and shrine, Clones, Monaghan.*

19. L'Île de Guesclan, Brittany, where Columbanus may have landed.

20. Chapel of Columbanus and site of great hall of Saxon palace, Cheddar, Somerset.

21. *Monk's cell and holy well, Penmon, Anglesey, north Wales.*

22. *Bardsey Island viewed from the Lleyn Peninsula, north Wales.*

23. *Culdee church of St Mary on the Rock, beyond the wall of St Andrews Cathedral, Fife, Scotland.*

Brendan sets out

In chapter two of the *Navigatio*, after hearing Barrind's story, Brendan chooses fourteen monks from his own community in Clonfert and tells them that he too wishes to sail to the Promised Land of the Saints. They eagerly volunteer to accompany him, and Brendan returns to his native Kerry in order to set out. As a good monk, he avoids visiting his parents, in obedience to Christ's challenge of turning one's back on father and mother for the sake of the gospel (Lk. 14. 26). Instead, Brendan and his monks pitch their tent beside a narrow creek under a mountain named Brendan's Seat. This was probably Brandon Creek, at the foot of Brandon Mountain, at the north-west end of the Dingle peninsula (*colour plate 11*). Here Brendan built a wooden-framed boat covered with oxhides. In the boat he and his fellow-monks put a mast and a sail, with supplies of food and water for forty days.

In Christian iconography, a boat symbolises the Church, in which we sail safely across life's stormy sea to heaven, much as Noah saved a remnant of the created world from drowning, and brought them safely to a new land lit by the rainbow of God's promise (Genesis 6–8). In Christian art, a ship's wooden mast symbolised the cross of Christ, raised aloft to speed the journey to our heavenly homeland.[8] For Celtic monks, curraghs of animal hide stretched over wooden ribs represented their human flesh bound to the wood of the cross. Monks wandered through the desert of the ocean in their frail skin crafts as true disciples of Christ. They could imitate the followers of Jesus in the storm-tossed boat who cried: 'Lord, save us, or we perish!' (Mt. 8. 25)

An allegory of monastic life

In the *Navigatio*, Brendan and his monks set sail towards the Promised Land and wander the ocean for seven years. The story is an allegory of monastic life with its annual cycle of labour and worship: they sail round in circles, and celebrate the great festivals in the same places each year.[9] A monastic steward appears at intervals with provisions for Brendan's monks; he explains that each year they will spend Holy Thursday on an island of sheep. Here they will roast a spotless lamb: this represents Jesus, the Lamb of God, who offered himself at the Last Supper.

They celebrate Easter on the back of a whale. We remember that the prophet Jonah spent three days in the belly of a whale before being spewed out to safety, and that Jesus used the story to symbolise his resurrection (Mt. 12. 40). They will spend from Easter to Pentecost in a paradise of birds, and Christmas in the monastery of St Ailbe. Each day is punctuated by the monastic liturgy: in their island paradise, the birds sing hymns and chant vespers and the other liturgical offices.

The birds on the Isle of Birds are the souls of angels who are not caught up in the fall of creation, and so they chant vespers in their songs, as the monks do. Since God creates everything, miracles are considered to be part of the natural world. Nature forms a backdrop to monastic life: in springtime, the daily pattern of the dawn chorus affirms the daily office of Lauds sung by the monks.[10] An island where birds sing the canonical hours derives from a Platonic concept: in the unfallen world, perfect music is heard, and for a monk, this would take the form of the monastic Office.

Egyptian desert language

The monks visit 'the place of choirs', where one of Brendan's monks stays behind, lured by their siren voices. They visit a 'delightful island' where monks 'swarm down to the shore like bees' to greet them. This image is taken from the account by the fourth-century Italian monk, Rufinus of Aquileia, recalling his stay in the Egyptian desert, which was described more fully in Chapter 1.

The *Navigatio* draws on themes from eastern texts which were popular in western monasteries by the seventh century: the *Life of Antony of Egypt* written by his friend Athanasius, the fourth-century *History of the Monks of Egypt*, the *Sayings* of the Desert Fathers, and the *Life of Paul* (of Thebes), a hermit whom Antony met, whose *Life* explores the contrast between the hermit and the community. Western monks probably combined these texts in compilations; their salient points would have become very familiar.[11]

The Faroes

When the unknown author of the *Navigatio* described an island of sheep and a paradise of birds, he drew his imagery from real nautical expeditions. A monk named Dicuil, who left Iona around 810 for the imperial court at Aachen, wrote a *Book of the Measurement of the Earth* fifteen years later. In the treatise, he described hermits who sailed from Ireland to settle on small islands, before the Norsemen laid them waste. Dicuil wrote that the islands were filled with countless sheep and very many different sorts of sea birds. He added: 'I have never found these islands mentioned in the authorities.'

These are likely to be the Faroes, past which monks sailed in order to find what lay to the far north: an island which they named Thule, in a frozen sea, where the sun never set. Geographically, this was Iceland, but Thule also symbolised the Promised Land, the heavenly Jerusalem which has no need of sun or moon, since 'the glory of God is its light' (Rev. 21. 23). The far north was understood to be the edge of the world, a mystical place where space and time slowed down, or even stopped.

The Faroes do not seem to have been discovered before 704, when Adomnán wrote his *Life of Columba*: he describes very many island locations, but not these. Within a hundred years, however, monks had reached the Faroes, for the *Voyage of Brendan*, written in the early 800s, includes accurate descriptions of life on these isles.

Thule

Dicuil wrote that a boat full of monks sailed from the Faroes in February to Thule, and stayed for several months, in order to watch the solstice, a time when the sun never sets. Brendan's *Navigatio* offers an unspoken comment that this was a futile quest, for one cannot reach Thule by one's own efforts. This was a profound theological question which Cassian posed to western monks, having observed the hermits of the eastern deserts: can monks gain salvation through hard work, at least in our fallen state?

The *Navigatio* contains a theology of the desert: ultimately, paradise is given to us as a gift. In the tale, we follow the monks' quest for an unknown desert, their discovery of a known desert, which is not as wonderful as they had hoped, and their return to normal life. It is a loving account, which also conveys that the entire voyage was pointless, since paradise can be experienced at home in one's monastery.[12]

The end of the world

Jesus told his disciples to preach the gospel to the ends of the earth, and then the final judgement would take place (Mt. 24. 14). Christians such as Patrick took this literally: they brought the good news of the Gospel to the end of the earth as they knew it, so that the Son of Man would come in glory, and earthly time would end, to be replaced by life in heaven.[13] The edge of the Western Sea was believed to be a significant place: it appeared to be 'the end of the earth'. Monks therefore asked: does the surrounding sea contain any more land? If not, have we reached the end of time?'

Monks chose to live in the 'desert' in order to be within sight of the Promised Land of heaven. The journey was a dangerous one, in which each monk struggled with inner and outer demons. The reader of the *Navigatio* is invited into this redemptive journey with some urgency, for Irish monks believed that the end of the world would come soon; the great Old Testament figures, Enoch and Elijah, would fight the antichrist, then all would die and rise to judgement. Reading the story, monks were reminded to be vigilant, for we know not the day nor the hour (Mt. 25. 13).

A monastic romance

The *Navigatio* is a monastic romance about God's love for humankind, in its struggle to attain the Promised Land of heaven. Brendan's voyage is our own; like the sailor monks, we await the adventure which is destined for each of us. We are warned not to initiate the perilous journey, but to await it. When Brendan was about to set sail, three monks came down to the beach and begged to be taken aboard. Brendan agreed, but foretold that two of them would meet a hideous fate, while the third would not return home. For Celtic monks, the virtue of stability did not mean staying in one place, but staying under the authority of one's abbot. The three monks lacked this virtue: they had not been asked to set out, and so were weak before the siren voices of temptation.

Like all good novels, Brendan's *Navigatio* contains a wealth of observed detail. The volcanoes of southern Iceland are described as a dangerous place where the monks were pelted with hot rocks. Islanders emerged from their forge and hurled great lumps of slag at the defenceless curragh. The whole island seemed on fire; the sea boiled as the molten lava broke its surface. Icebergs become pillars of crystal floating in the sea. The *Navigatio* describes how Brendan saw an enormous column of bright crystal and sailed towards it for three days, his boat enmeshed in silver pack-ice that was harder than marble. The water was clear as glass; even in the iceberg's shadow, the monks could feel the sun's heat.

Eventually, like Barrind before him, Brendan reaches the Promised Land. Yet since this is a story of finite monastic life, Brendan is told to return home with some of the heavenly fruit and precious stones, since his last days are near. He returns to his own community, who receive him joyfully. He warns them of his approaching death, receives the sacraments and dies among his brother monks.

Brandon Mountain

Brendan became an immensely popular saint, particularly in his native Kerry. Towering above Brandon Creek, Brendan's point of departure in the *Navigatio*, Brandon Mountain became a centre for pilgrimage, perhaps as early as the eighth century. At the mountain peak are remains of cells, a chapel and a holy well. Each July, reviving an earlier tradition, pilgrims climb the mountain to visit the shrine at its summit.

The western end of the Dingle peninsula became a sacred landscape honouring Brendan. Over 400 beehive-shaped stone huts are found here, perhaps built as shelters for pilgrims. There are also numerous churches, ogham-inscribed stones and pillars decorated with crosses. A 'Saints' Road' led from

Ventry Harbour on the south side of the peninsula to the summit of Brandon Mountain. Pilgrims evidently arrived by sea before walking the 12-mile route that led up the mountain.[14]

Gallarus Oratory

Gallarus Oratory overlooks Smerwick Harbour, near the western end of the Dingle peninsula. It is the only complete early medieval chapel on the mainland; its shape has been compared with that of an upturned boat. A banked wall demarcates the monastery in which it stood, and an inner wall separates the remains of the monks' huts from the chapel. The building perhaps dates from the eighth century and is made from local gritstone. The little church is constructed with unmortared stones, each layer set further inwards, to form a curved roof. Its nine ridge stones are still intact. Often a corbelled roof of this design collapses in the middle, its weakest point, unless its masons are exceptionally skilled. Such chapels are almost all found in Kerry.[15]

The oratory has a low doorway at its western end, with two large lintel stones. A wooden or leather door hung from a pair of projecting stones inside the chapel. At its eastern end, a small circular window splays inwards, to shed morning light on the missal, for the priest to celebrate the Eucharist. We can imagine eager, if weary, pilgrims gathered outside to receive the sacrament, before starting their climb up Brandon Mountain, where they would visit Brendan's shrine at its summit.

Gallarus Oratory, Dingle peninsula, Kerry.

Kilmalkedar

A mile north of Gallarus Oratory near the western end of the Dingle peninsula, Kilmalkedar (or *Cill Mhaoilchédair*), is one of the few sites in the area which was not taken over by the cult of Brendan; it is dedicated to a local saint of the Corra Dhuibhne named Maolcéthair who died around 636; he may have been an Ulster prince. The present church is twelfth-century Romanesque, with arcading modelled on Cormac's Chapel at Cashel; on its roof a finial survives at the apex of the gable.

There are considerable earlier remains from Maolcéthair's monastery: an early eighth-century pillar stone inside the church has the Latin alphabet carved on it, and was probably used to teach literacy to students. To the west of the church, along its ancient causeway, is the graveyard with a simple high cross. At the churchyard entrance is an ogham-inscribed stone; there are remains of a cell, and also a finely carved sundial. St Paul wrote that when time reached its fullness, God sent his Son (Galatians 4. 4); a sundial enabled monks to mark the time now, in the final age, awaiting Christ's return in glory. By indicating when to chant the daytime Offices, the sundial enabled monks to join in the worship of heaven.[16]

High cross and Romanesque church, Kilmalkedar, Kerry.

Celtic sundial, Kilmalkedar, Kerry.

8

THE COLUMBAN FAMILY

Perhaps the most outstanding of the Celtic monks, Columba (521–597) was a warrior and politician, a scholar, priest and poet who played an important role in both Irish and Scottish history. Columba (or *Columcille* in Irish), whose name means 'dove', was born into the royal family of the Northern Uí Néill at Gartan, near Letterkenny in Donegal, according to the Old Irish *Life of Columba* (or *Betha Coluim Cille*). Columba began his schooling under the care of a foster father, a priest named Cruithnecan: this suggests that he was intended for the Church at an early age. Columba also studied under a Christian bard in his mother's country of Leinster. He became a monk at a young age, and was ordained as a deacon in the monastery of Finnian at Movilla.

Later he was ordained a priest, and in about 546 he founded his first monastery at Derry in his family's territory, on land given to him by his tribe. He established various other communities: those claiming him as founder include Kells (Meath), Swords (near Dublin), Drumcliffe (Sligo), Moone (Kildare), Tory Island (Donegal) and Durrow (Offaly), among others. Durrow and Iona are the only Columban foundations mentioned by Bede.

Irish accounts of Columba relate how on a visit to his former abbot, Finnian of Movilla, Columba borrowed a book from the library and secretly copied it at night. He was discovered when he had almost finished, and Finnian demanded the copy. This first recorded breach of copyright was brought to trial before the High King, who ruled in Finnian's favour.

Durrow

Columba perhaps established a monastery at Durrow around 556, in his mid-thirties; it became the most important Columban foundation before the Iona community transferred to Kells in the early ninth century, and always claimed seniority to Iona. The *Annals of Tigernach* relates that the land was granted to Columba by 'Aedh, son of Brendan, King of Tebtha'. Early sources relate that when Columba sailed to Argyll, he appointed Cormac Ua Liathain as prior of Durrow, but owing to rivalries between the northern and southern clans, Cormac was unable to retain his position. He fled from the monastery, leaving in charge a first cousin of Columba, Laisrén, who was acceptable to both parties.

Bede dates its foundation to the period before Columba left Ireland in 563; he describes it as *monasterium nobile in Hibernia*. The monastery was often ravaged by Vikings, and was destroyed by the Normans. However, it retained its importance: at a later period, Armagh and Durrow were called the 'univer-sities of the West'. The abbey was dissolved in the sixteenth century. The site includes a large enclosure, five early Christian grave slabs, a very fine high cross dating from the mid-ninth century, remains of other crosses, and the monastery's well (*colour plate 13*).

The magnificent *Book of Durrow* was created between 650 and 700, either at Durrow, or at Lindisfarne or Iona. It was perhaps taken to Durrow by British monks fleeing from the Vikings, some time before 916. It pre-dates the *Book of Kells* by over a century, and is the earliest surviving fully decorated insular Gospel book. Its artist was unused to depicting human figures, but was more familiar with animal forms. The book contains highly detailed carpet pages, filled with curvilinear designs and interlaced animals; it is now in Trinity College, Dublin.

High cross, Durrow, Offaly.

Durrow was formerly known as *Dairmag*, 'the Plain of the oaks', which may refer to a sacred oak grove; some of the few remaining pre-medieval Irish oak trees are to be found here. The avenue of oaks lining the fields beside the abbey mark the route of the ancient highway of Ireland. The site is just off the N52, 5 miles north of Tullamore, down a drive to the left of the road.

Iona

Columba sailed to Scotland as a 'pilgrim for Christ'. As a successful warrior-prince, politician and abbot, Columba may also have been invited by his relative Conall, the new king of Dalriada (or Argyll), to help him repel the Picts. One tradition relates that Columba was given the island of Iona by King Conall, as a site for a monastery. Iona is 3 miles long, and lies west of the larger island of Mull.

We know a considerable amount about life in Columba's community, because in about 690 the ninth abbot of Iona, Adomnán, wrote a *Life of Columba* and preserved for us many details of daily life on the island. The earliest surviving text of the *Life* was written on Iona by Dorbbéne, a monk who succeeded Adomnán as abbot and died in 713. We are fortunate to possess such an early copy, written on goatskin parchment in a heavy Irish hand.

Life on Iona

Columba lived in a hut built on planks on a small rocky mound in the monastery compound. The mound can still be seen in front of the large Benedictine abbey that was later built on the site. The mound may also be the 'little hill overlooking the monastery' from which, according to Adomnán, Columba gave his final blessing to the monks before his death.[1]

Adomnán describes the monks walking across the island with their farm implements on their backs, to reach the sandy plain where they grew crops. He tells us of the white horse that carried the milk churns from the cow pasture, and he mentions expeditions to larger islands to fetch wood for building, since there were no trees on Iona. Adomnán pictures the monks writing manuscripts, and praying in the small church, where Columba's clear voice could be heard above the others. He could also be recognised by his white cowl, or hooded cloak, for the other monks wore unbleached cowls.

The *Life* refers to fifty-five sea voyages back and forth between Iona and Ireland. Monks and pilgrims came to visit or to join the community. Those travelling from Scotland crossed the island of Mull and then shouted across the Sound to Iona, for a brother to ferry them over. From his hut on planks, Columba could see them coming. He acquired neighbouring islands to provide necessary resources for the monastery: the monks grew grain on the islands of Coll and Tiree ('Barley Island'). His uncle, Ernán, was prior of a community on the island of Jura to the south-east, where his mother, Eithne, is also said to have established a convent.

Early remains

Today there are few remains of Iona's Celtic monastery; St Odhráin's chapel is the earliest building to survive on the island. It dates from the twelfth century, and stands within what was probably the first Christian burial ground on Iona. It is named after an early monk who may have lived here before Columba's arrival. Odhráin's oratory resembles Irish chapels of the period, with a single doorway in the west wall, decorated with chevron and beak-head ornament. It was probably rebuilt as a family burial vault by Somerled, King of the Isles, who died in 1164.[2]

In 1979, excavations were carried out in the early seventh-century boundary ditch between the little hill on which Columba's cell was built and Odhráin's cemetery. Objects were discovered which would have been in use at the end of Columba's lifetime, including heeled shoes and other leather goods, and elegant wooden bowls that had been turned on a lathe in the monastic work-shops. Clay moulds indicated that fine quality metalwork was produced. There had also been a glass furnace in which glass beads were created, and orna-ments of various colours with twisted patterns.[3]

The great rectangular ramparts which surrounded the monastery on Iona can still be traced: they were constructed around the time of Columba's death, and were partly enhanced by an impenetrable hedge of hawthorn and holly.

Entrance to early cemetery, Iona.

The tiny chapel in front of the Benedictine abbey is also built on Celtic foundations, and may mark the site of Columba's shrine. There are three elaborate
high crosses, and a winding path of large stones, known as the 'Street of the
Dead'. Chieftains were brought to Iona from the Scottish mainland for burial,
and this was the track along which they were solemnly carried.

Outside the great rampart, 1000ft to the north-east, are the remains of
a Celtic cemetery, named *Cladh an Disirt* in Gaelic. It was entered through
an impressive gateway framed by two large stone pillars; these supported a
giant lintel, which has now fallen. The cemetery was enclosed by a wall, and
beside it was a hermitage, whose superior is named in a twelfth-century list of
monastic officials. There are the remains of a medieval stone chapel beside the
entrance to the cemetery.[4]

Columba lived on Iona for thirty-five years. He returned to Ireland in 575
after an absence of twelve years, to attend an assembly of the Uí Néill clan
at Druimm-Cete in Derry, as adviser to Áedán, the new king of Dalriada. The
assembly agreed to Dalriada's independence from Ireland. The standing of the
Irish bards was also discussed, and Columba argued in their favour.

Drumcliffe

It was during this visit to Ireland that Columba is likely to have established a
monastery at Drumcliffe, 5 miles north of Sligo city; the site is now bisected
by the N15. It is dramatically situated in the narrow coastal plain between the
almost vertical slope of Ben Bulben and the sea. Drumcliffe is close to the site
of the Battle of *Cul-Dreimhne*, which took place at the foot of Ben Bulben
in 561, two years before Columba sailed to Argyll. The *Annals of the Four
Masters* inform us that this took place in revenge for the killing of a hostage
prince who was under the protection of Columba. Although he was successful, it may be that Columba was wounded in the battle: Adomnán refers to his
battle scar, tactfully suggesting that it was inflicted by an angel.[5]

The monastery was founded on land donated to Columba by a local king;
later *coarbs* of the monastery (guardians who were responsible for administration) were members of Columba's family, the Cenél Conaill. In 1267 the
monastery suffered extensive damage by fire. The community is frequently
mentioned in Irish annals until the thirteenth century when it began to decline,
and its churches were plundered and robbed.[6]

Excavation of the early monastic site has uncovered a wide range of
animal, fish and bird remains, together with seeds of cereals and other
plants. Hearths and storage pits indicated considerable domestic activity, and
there were cultivation ridges where crops were grown. Craftsmen fashioned
items of iron and bronze, antler and bone.[7] An ancient path leads from the
monastery to the river. One finds it by proceeding northwards along the

main road from the round tower: the first track on the left leads down to the tidal Drumcliffe River estuary, where monks could set sail at high tide, and so go out to sea.

Monastic remains

The chief visible remains are a ruined round tower and two high crosses: a fragment of a plain cross, and a fine tenth-century high cross, on whose east face are carvings of Adam and Eve, Cain and Abel, Daniel in the lions' den and Christ in glory (*colour plate 12*). Carved on its west face are the Presentation of Christ in the temple, two figures and the Crucifixion. The cross is also decorated with fabulous beasts and interlacing patterns.

The tower was built between 900 and 1200; it survives to a height of only 27ft. Its doorway was high above ground level and faced east, perhaps towards the doorway of the monastery's principal church. The round tower was struck by lightning in 1396; in the eighteenth or nineteenth century much of it was demolished and the stone was used to construct the nearby bridge.[8]

The monster in the loch

Columba returned to Ireland ten years later, in 585, to visit his monastery at Durrow, and that of Ciarán at Clonmacnoise. His enthusiastic welcome there by Abbot Alither was described in Chapter 6. Columba twice travelled north to Inverness, probably on political missions to confer with Brude, King of the Picts. His first visit was apparently to negotiate peace between King Conall and the Picts, and to ask permission to settle on Iona, which King Brude considered to be in Pictish territory. Columba and his companions sailed up the Great Glen to Inverness, and Adomnán recounts that on the journey they encountered a creature in the River Ness that people have equated with the Loch Ness monster. A local person who died after being bitten by the monster was being buried near the bank of Loch Ness. Disregarding their experience, Columba told one of his monks to sail across the loch and retrieve a boat. The account proceeds:

> Lugne mocu-Min obeyed without delay, and taking off his clothes except his tunic plunged into the water. But the monster, whose hunger had not been satisfied earlier, was lurking in the depths of the river, keen for more prey. Feeling the water disturbed by his swimming, it suddenly swam to the surface, and with a mighty roar from its gaping mouth it sped towards the man as he swam in midstream.[9]

Columba ordered the monster to return to the depths, and the monk reached the safety of the boat.

Columba's death

Columba died on Iona. Adomnán describes the abbot's final tour of the island, when he was pulled in a cart, since he could no longer walk far. He blessed the island, the monks, the barns and the white horse. He returned to his hut and tried to complete a psalm that he was copying, but was unable to do so. That night was Whitsun Eve. Columba went to church for the midnight office, but collapsed there and died. Adomnán described his last hours:

> At midnight he rose up in haste at the ringing of the bell and went to the church, and he ran ahead of the others and entered alone; and kneeling in prayer he sank down beside the altar. Diormit, his attendant … entered the church and cried in a tearful voice: 'Where are you, father, where are you?' And groping through the darkenss, as the brothers' lamps had not yet been brought, he found the saint lying before the altar, and lifting him up a little and sitting beside him, put his holy head in his lap.
>
> Meanwhile, the assembled monks ran up with lights, and began to lament at the sight of their dying father. And, as we have learned from some who were present, while his soul had not yet departed the saint opened and raised his eyes, and looked round on both sides with a wonderfully cheerful and joyous expression … Diormit then raised [Columba's] right hand to bless the saint's company of monks … And after his holy blessing, signified in this way, he at once breathed his last.[10]

His monks prayed around him for three days before burying him. They were left to grieve in peace, since storms prevented visitors from crossing the Sound.

From Columba's time onwards, Iona was considered to be the centre of Celtic learning. Irish monks came to Iona to study and pray, as did Irish-trained monks from across Europe. Meanwhile brothers from Iona played a leading part in the spread of Christianity among the Picts of eastern Scotland and the Anglo-Saxons of Northumbria. The Columban monastery of Lindisfarne was founded by Aidan, a monk from Iona, and these two communities became focal points of the Columban family, its cultural traditions and its manuscript art.

Kells

After Columba's death, Iona suffered a number of Norse raids. In 806, during their third attack, Vikings killed sixty-eight monks, and the abbot of Iona then took his monks to a safer location in Ireland. This was Kells in Meath: it was 25 miles inland, and therefore better protected from Norse raids. This may have been a new monastic site; it became the headquarters of the Columban monastic family network. From then on, the abbot of Kells was called

The south cross, Kells, Meath.

Round tower and unfinished east cross, Kells, Meath.

'the successor of Columba'. Kells is in the valley of the Blackwater, 20 miles west of Drogheda, near to the intersection of the N3 and N52.

Outside the cathedral, four high crosses survive from the Celtic monastery. The south cross was probably erected soon after the monks arrived from Iona. It is inscribed 'the Cross of Patrick and Columba', and stands beside a tenth-century round tower, into which the monks could climb for safety, drawing their ladder up after them. The tower is 92ft high, and must have been frequently used for, despite its inland location, the monastery at Kells was plundered at least seven times before 1006. Most round towers have four windows at the top, so that the monks could keep watch in all directions. Unusually, this example contains five windows, each facing one of the five ancient roads that lead to Kells. The unfinished east cross dates from the twelfth century, and shows how plain panels were prepared first, and carvings were executed later.

To the north-west of the cathedral is Columba's House, which may date from the eleventh century. It is a small church with a basement, through which one enters the building, and walls over 4ft thick. The church has a steeply pitched roof, and between the barrel vault and the roof is an attic or croft divided into three rooms, where monks could work and sleep. One can climb up a steep ladder into the croft: it is not difficult to imagine the monks sleeping comfortably above their little church. This may be one of the few buildings that have survived intact from early times. It is kept locked, but the key is held at no. 27, down the road.

The Book of Kells

When the monks fled from Iona, they brought their treasures with them including, perhaps, the *Book of Kells*, a magnificently decorated gospel book, which was created on Iona around 800. Its text is a poor version of the Latin gospels; it is interesting that its scholarship does not match the skill lavished on its illustrations. These were executed in the latest Northumbrian style by monks trained at Lindisfarne. When Kells was plundered in 1006, the gospel book was stolen and buried for three months. It was retrieved, but had lost its jewel-encrusted cover. It is now in the library of Trinity College, Dublin.

Skreen

Skreen is the site of a Columban monastery, 12 miles south-west of Drogheda and 2 miles east-north-east of Tara. It was originally known as Achall, until

875 when the shrine and relics of Columba were brought for safety to the monastery. The site then became known as *Scrin Choluim Chille* ('Columba's Shrine') or, more simply, *An Scrin* ('The Shrine'). The monastery was plundered several times between the late tenth and thirteenth centuries. The shrine itself was stolen in 1027, but was later recovered. The present ruined church may date from the fifteenth century. To the north-east of the church is a late medieval stone cross whose stumpy arms may have had wooden extensions; the Crucifixion is carved on its west face.

Late-medieval cross, Skreen, Meath.

Moone

A number of Irish monasteries formed part of the Columban family, although their connection with Columba is uncertain. One of these is Moone Abbey (*Mhainister Mhaoine*) in Kildare; it is situated above the River Greese, a tributary of the River Barrow. Moone is referred to as *Maen Colmcille* ('Columba's property') in a twelfth-century literary source and in the fifteenth-century *Book of Lismore*. The nearby well, which is dedicated to Columba, was a popular place of annual pilgrimage until the nineteenth century. The O'Flanagan family provided the monastery's hereditary abbots until the eleventh century, and in about 1225 the archbishop of Dublin gave the monastery's lands and mill to St Patrick's Cathedral, Dublin.[11]

In the abbey grounds there is a magnificent ninth-century high cross: it is 23ft high, the second tallest in Ireland. The granite for the cross was brought from some miles away; its three stone sections are of slightly different hues. It is carved in flat relief, and was probably painted, to resemble the stylised figures on metalwork of the time, which were decorated with multicoloured enamels. It is the only known work by this sculptor.

The central panel of its west face depicts the crucifixion: according to tradition, Christ on the cross faced west, the direction of sunset, death and the kingdom of darkness. Beneath the crucifixion scene, Adam and Eve face one another, separated by the serpent coiled around the tree of life. Lower still, Abraham sacrifices Isaac: he is seated and raises his sword, while Isaac lays his head on the altar, but above Isaac, we can see the ram which will be slain instead. At the base of the cross, six hungry lions paw at the prophet Daniel, who has been thrown into their den.

The base of the north face of the cross depicts loaves and fishes: this refers to the miracle in which Jesus fed several thousand people

Adam and Eve, Abraham and Isaac, and Daniel: high cross, Moone, Kildare.

in the desert. The fish resemble those found in the Sea of Galilee rather than those seen in Irish waters; this suggests that the sculptor was familiar with Near Eastern models.[12] There are similar depictions of the loaves and fishes on other high crosses in the Barrow Valley, including the two crosses at Castledermot (see Chapter 1) in which, unusually, Christ is depicted beside the loaves and fishes, poised to bless and multiply them. Moone is off the N9 between Kildare and Carlow. To find it, drive to the centre of Moone village; proceed between two high stone columns down the drive to the abbey.

Gleanncholmcille

Finally we will consider a remote valley in north-west Donegal where a group of early hermits fostered devotion to Columba (*colour plate 14*). It was the agricultural wealth of Gleanncholmcille and its surrounding valleys which attracted the farmers who built magnificent court tombs here around 3000 BC, with an open court and burial galleries inside a large, coffin-shaped cairn. The climate was then milder and there was more land to farm, before peat bog started to cover the valleys and hillsides a thousand years before Christ.[13]

Even today, Gleanncholmcille has a mild micro-climate: bluebells grow unexpectedly out of the bog around Columba's Chapel in late June, and the tiny magenta bog pea is in flower where one climbs to Columba's well, while arum lilies flourish beside the small homes of local people. Peat is cut and dried through the summer for use in winter. Early cultivation terraces suggest that hermits grew cereals and herbs, as they did at similar Irish foundations. The later castles and post-Norman religious houses found elsewhere in Ireland are not present in this remote area of Donegal; it is likely that an early Christian way of life continued in this region until many Irish were driven westwards by the Plantation of Ulster in 1609.

A number of early saints established hermitages in this remote north-western region of Ireland. In Chapter 2, we heard how Assicus, Patrick's favourite disciple and metalworker, may have lived as a hermit on Rathlin O'Birne Island, 10 miles south-west of Gleanncholmcille. The hermitage of a distant cousin and contemporary of Columba, Aed Mac Bricne, who was a great grandson of Niall of the Nine Hostages, survives 10 miles south-east of Gleanncholmcille, high up on Slieve League, with remains of a rectangular church, a beehive cell, a tall pillar with an incised cross and three holy wells.[14]

The pilgrimage

The *turas*, (literally, 'tour', journey or pilgrimage) round the valley of Gleanncholmcille began early: a number of the stations have standing stones with elaborate crosses carved in a local style which may date from between

500 and 700. The pilgrimage as it is performed today is about 3 miles long, crossing the valley floor twice, and climbing steeply to Columba's well.

This may be a combination of two earlier *turas*, one around the monastic site on the valley floor, and another centred upon an early hermitage below Columba's well, on the valley's northern slope. The crosses at the stations in the valley floor are larger and more elaborately carved; some of their designs resemble those carved elsewhere in stone and metal dating from around 700.[15]

The modern Church of Ireland church stands within a circular enclosure, with a number of early Christian grave slabs towards its east end. Running east and west beneath the centre of the enclosure is a *souterrain*, or series of underground chambers, which incorporate several early Christian grave stones carved with crosses: they serve as a roof slab, a corbel, a lintel and an upright prop, and were probably built into the *souterrain* about or after 700.[16] The early monastery was located at a pre-Christian holy site: what is probably a Neolithic court tomb, dating from around 3000 BC, adjoins the west wall of the churchyard, and one begins the *turas* at the mouth of the court tomb, which was evidently enlarged and converted into the *souterrain*.

Station 2 of the *turas* is 160ft west along the road, and is marked by a decorated cross-pillar, standing on a rectangular *leacht*, or dry-stone wall altar, on a small outcrop of rock (*colour plate 15*). The pilgrimage then winds round the valley. Station 15, the final station is again inside the churchyard, at a cross-pillar of schist; its upper third has broken off. Its unusual design includes a pair of knots at what was its midpoint.

Cross pillar at station 15, Gleanncholmcille, Donegal.

Tomb shrine and healing stones, Columba's Chapel, Gleanncholmcille, Donegal.

Columba's Chapel

The stations on the northern valley slope are centred around Columba's Chapel, a rectangular stone building with a doorway. Inside its north-east wall is Columba's Bed, which appears to be an early tomb shrine, delineated by slabs set on their edges, and covered by two large flat slabs. Three round stones were kept in a small chamber in the wall above the shrine, and were often sent out of the Glen, even as far away as America, to cure people.

Outside the chapel are three cairns of stones, each topped with a small cross slab. A cairn, or pile of stones, often commemorated a dead person. There is a circular dry-stone wall enclosure around the chapel and cairns. Beyond the enclosure are the remains of a collapsed circular stone hut, before one reaches a second enclosure containing another cairn topped with a cross. There are ancient cultivation terraces on the slopes below the enclosure.[17] It is likely that this is where an early hermit lived, and where he possibly died and was buried.

Colmumba's holy well is on the hill slope above the hermitage complex. The well house is built of dry-stone walls, above which stands a carved cross with rudimentary arms. Pilgrims bring three stones to the well, one for each of three circuits of the *turas*, and over hundreds of years the stones have come to form an enormous L-shaped cairn, over 100ft long. It is mute evidence to the fact that this is one of Ireland's most ancient pilgrimage sites, where Christians have come to pray for almost 1500 years.

View through the doorway of Columba's Chapel towards the central cairn of three within the enclosure, Gleanncholmcille, Donegal.

9

THREE SOUTHERN ABBOTS

olumba established what was to become an extensive monastic family. Meanwhile, other saints founded communities whose influence was confined to the region of its founder. In this chapter, we will focus on three monks in southern Ireland whose lives spanned the seventh century: Kevin of Glendalough, Colmán of Kilmacduagh and Moling of St Mullins. Sources concerning their lives are quite late, but there are considerable early remains at each of their chief foundations, which enable us to glimpse how they lived and worked.

Kevin

Kevin was a contemporary of Ciarán of Clonmacnoise (see Chapter 6). Both men founded a settlement beside an important route across Ireland, and both monasteries later grew in size and importance. But while Clonmacnoise overlooks flat meadows and the broad, winding Shannon, Glendalough is in very different terrain, beside a pass through the Wicklow Mountains. Its name, *Gleann-dá-loch*, means 'Glen of the two lakes', and it is in an outstandingly beautiful location, 25 miles south of Dublin and 12 miles inland.

Unlike Ciarán of Clonmacnoise, Kevin appears to have lived into old age. The two communities developed links in the tenth century; there are remains of a church dedicated to Ciarán at Glendalough. Kevin's Latin *Life* describes him travelling west across Ireland to visit Ciarán at Clonmacnoise as the young man lay stricken with the plague, but relates that Ciarán died before the older monk's arrival.

Kevin's *Lives*

Kevin (d. *c.* 618) was born in the early sixth century, of a noble Leinster family ousted from kingship. His name, *Cóemhghein*, means 'fairborn'. There are six surviving *Lives* of Kevin, three in Latin and three in Irish. The earliest appears to have been written by a monk at Glendalough in the tenth or eleventh century, since he refers to Dublin as a powerful and warlike city of men who were hardy fighters and most skilful with ships; this describes a city under Viking control.

We do not know where Kevin was educated; he was said to have been trained by three wise old monks. When searching for a deserted place in which to stay, he came to Glendalough and lived beside the Upper Lake in the hollow of a tree. Later he was ordained a priest by a bishop named Lugidus, who sent him out with some monks to found a new church in an unidentified place. Here he spent some time 'gathering servants for Christ' before moving with them to Glendalough.

Glendalough

According to his Latin *Lives*, Kevin founded a great monastery in the lower part of the valley where two clear rivers flow together. Once the community was established, he entrusted it to the care of responsible monks and retired to the upper valley, a mile to the west, to live once more as a hermit. Here he built a small dwelling in a narrow place between the mountain and the lake, where there were dense woods and clear streams.

This area is known as *Díseart Kevin* (Kevin's Desert). It is a beautiful location, particularly when the early morning sun begins to warm the south-eastern corner of the Upper Lake, where Kevin built his 'desert' or hermitage (*colour plate 3*). He was said to have fed on sorrel and nettles. Beside the shore, sorrel of unusually fine quality still grows; nettle broth was considered a valuable food at this time, and sorrel soup is still prized.

On a promontory overlooking the Upper Lake, the remains of a circular hut known as Kevin's Cell have been excavated, and there are possible sites of other huts further up the hillside. There is an early church, *Teampaill na Skellig*, on a shelf above the Upper Lake, close to 'St Kevin's Bed', a cave in the rock face which may have been a Bronze Age mineshaft.[1] According to tradition, Kevin used this as a shelter.

The Reefert Church

The Poulanass river cascades down the hillside into the Upper Lake on its southern shore, and not far from the river is the Reefert Church, in a grove of hazel trees. This appears to have been a church used by the solitary monks who chose to live in Kevin's Desert. When a number of monks withdrew to a 'desert' away from the main monastic site, a superior might be appointed to take charge of their settlement.

Early graves, Reefert Church, Glendalough, Wicklow.

The Reefert Church is a fine eleventh-century building with an early example of a chancel arch. A large stone with four interlinked crosses may have been an altar front; it is now in St Kevin's church in the monastic city. The graveyard is one of the few in which Celtic grave markers are still in their original position, lying flat on the graves, with other slabs and small crosses serving as upright headstones.[2]

An inscription on one tombstone reads: 'A prayer for Caibre, son of Cathail.' According to the annals, Caibre was a hermit of Glendalough who died in 1013. The name Reefert appears to derive from *Righ Fearta*, or 'burial place of kings'. The title may date from the late-twelfth century when the royal family of the O'Tooles was driven from Kildare into the Wicklow Mountains by the Normans. Reefert was known as the Princes' Church in the eighteenth century.

The monastic city

After some years as a hermit beside the Upper Lake, Kevin apparently returned to the monastic city to die. We are told that he sent a party of monks to the hermitage to pray for him, and that his burial place was 'to the east of the Lower Lake'. This appears to indicate St Mary's church, at the western end of the monastic city. This is one of the earliest churches on the site; in the eighteenth century it was still venerated as the place of Kevin's burial. Its chancel was probably built in the tenth century, but its nave is considerably earlier. After his death, Kevin was succeeded as abbot by his nephew Molibba, who appears to have been the first bishop of Glendalough.

The monastery is set on higher ground, above the confluence of the River Glendasan and the River Glenealo. It is a common opinion that the monks moved to this location only after Kevin's death, but it is equally possible that Kevin chose this site. As we saw, his original foundation was said to have been 'where two clear rivers flow together', at a distance from Kevin's Desert.[3]

The lower site at Glendalough is extensive, with remains of five churches and a round tower. Another two churches were later built further down the valley. The main entrance to the monastery is close to the road where it crosses the Glendasan River. The present bridge may stand on the site of an earlier one which the annals describe as being swept away in the great flood of 1177.

The enclosure is approached by a gateway, the only surviving monastic entrance in Ireland. The impressive building dates from some time after 900. Two fine granite arches survive; its *antae*, or projecting walls at each end, suggest that there was a timber roof. The outline of a large, simple cross is carved on a giant slab beyond the inner arch. This marked out the monastery as a place of sanctuary, where criminals could take refuge from the law. Beneath the arches are preserved the large paving slabs of the original causeway into the monastic city.[4]

In time the monastery would have contained workshops, scriptoria for manuscript writing and copying, guest houses and an infirmary, farm buildings

St Kevin's church, Glendalough, Wicklow.

and dwellings both for monks and for craftsmen and labourers, together with their families. The site was above flood level and on fertile soil, with woodland bordering the Glenealo river to the south. The hillside is named Derrybawn, from the Gaelic for 'white oak wood'. The white-leaved oak was particularly revered; it also provided valuable fuel, and oak was durable timber for building. The oak galls may have been used to make black ink, and herds of pigs from the monastery would have foraged for acorns.[5]

St Kevin's Church

St Kevin's Church is the best-preserved building within the enclosure. Its steeply pitched stone roof is built on the corbel principle, like the beehive huts of Kerry; each stone slopes slightly outwards to throw off the rain. There is a first floor with a loft above, in which monks may have slept. A small round tower is built into the west gable; a similar belfry was constructed at Trinity church, further down the valley, but it collapsed during a storm in 1818.

The small sacristy adjoining St Kevin's church was perhaps built in the twelfth century, when a chancel was also added. In 1779, when the antiquarian Gabriel Béranger visited the site, there was an altar of stones and sods in the chancel. Eucharist was celebrated here during the pattern, or patronal feast of Kevin on 3 June. From about 1810, Sunday Mass was held here. The chancel was later destroyed; its foundations are visible beside the sacristy.[6]

The cathedral and round tower

At the centre of the monastic city is the cathedral, a large building constructed over several hundred years from the ninth century onwards. It is referred to in the annals as 'the abbey', and was an imposing building: its nave is wider than that of any other early Irish church. Outside it stands a tall ringed cross of granite.

The round tower dominates the monastic city. Although it is built at the bottom of the valley, it can be seen by travellers approaching from every direction. It is about 100ft high, and a watchman at the top could spot attackers advancing from either end of the valley, or over the mountains. At the top, four windows face the compass points; beneath were six floors, four of them each lit by a tiny window. Since a monastery served as a sanctuary not only for people but also for goods and cattle, looting was frequent. Glendalough is first recorded as being burnt in 770. Over the next 400 years, annals note its destruction on nineteen occasions. Danes attacked nine times, Irish plunderers once, and three times there were accidental fires.

Round tower at dawn, Glendalough, Wicklow.

A centre for pilgrimage

During the twelfth-century reforms of the Irish Church, Glendalough was handed over to a group of Augustinian canons, but it was destroyed several times, and finally suppressed in the sixteenth century. Pilgrims continued to visit the site, especially to celebrate St Kevin's feast day. In 1873, William Wilde wrote that as a youth he had often attended the celebration, when great crowds of people camped among the ruins. Before dawn there was a procession up the Glendasan River with sick children, to dip them into a pool named Kevin's Keeve; this was later adapted for a saw mill. Stone crosses at various points in the valley may mark stations on the pilgrims' route. The procession ended beside the Upper Lake, in Kevin's Desert.[7] There is now a small retreat centre beside the road above the monastic city, and hermitages where once again people can come to experience the solitude and beauty of the valley.

Colmán of Kilmacduagh

There were some 300 Celtic saints named Colmán, a word meaning 'little dove'. Colmán of Kilmacduagh (d. *c.* 632) was born in the mid-sixth century. According to late texts, he was the son of Duac, an Irish chieftain (mac Duach means 'son of Duac'). He trained in Enda's monastery on Inis Mór: his ruined church in the tiny settlement of Kilmurvey, *Teampaill Mac Duach*, is illustrated in Chapter 3. Colmán later returned to Clare, where he lived on an austere diet of vegetables and water in a cave in the Burren Hills, together with a disciple. He was unwillingly consecrated a bishop.

Colmán later founded the monastery of Kilmacduagh on land given to him by his kinsman, Guaire the Generous, King of Connaght. Guaire lived in the nearby town of Gort, and provided the workmen and materials to build Colmán's monastery. Legends about Colmán tell how a cockerel used to wake him in time for the night office, a mouse prevented him from going to sleep during his silent vigil afterwards, and a fly kept the place in his prayer book. Part of Colmán's crosier is in Dublin, in the National Museum of Ireland.

Colmán's monastery

Kilmacduagh, 17 miles south of Galway, is one of the finest Irish monastic sites, set in green meadows near the shore of a lough, with the Burren Hills on the horizon. The cathedral is the largest building in the monastic enclosure: it occupies the site of a rectangular seventh-century church. The west end, with its lintelled doorway, roof corbels and steeply pitched gable, was probably built before the eleventh century.[8] Colmán is said to be buried in a shrine outside the cathedral.

Nearby, the ruined church of St John the Baptist dates from the tenth century. Remains of Our Lady's church stand beside the road that was driven through the site in the eighteenth century. Next to St John's church, the Glebe House was the later bishop's residence. From an upstairs oriel window, the bishop used to bless pilgrims who gathered here on Colmán's feast day, 29 October.[9]

The round tower

The most striking feature of the site is a tenth-century round tower, 100ft high. It is the tallest in Ireland, and leans 2ft out of perpendicular. This is probably because it lacks deep foundations: it was built on soft earth, on the site of an early Christian burial ground. When the tower was restored in the late-nineteenth century, skeletons were found lying oriented east to west beneath the centre of the tower and below its walls. The tower had seven timber floors, where many people could take refuge.

Round tower, Kilmacduagh, Galway.

The lowest portion of the tower was found to be filled with large and small stones; above this, human bones found in a deposit of ash provided evidence of a disastrous fire. Copper fragments suggested that monks had taken refuge in the tower, taking their precious church vessels with them.[10] Viking raiders plundered the site in the tenth century, and the monastery was destroyed by Normans in the thirteenth. It was restored by the local chieftain and by Augustinian canons; its cemetery continues to be used by families from the surrounding area.

Moling

The cult of Moling (d. *c.* 697) was early and widespread. Moling came from a noble Leinster family and became a monk at Glendalough. He later founded his own monastery at St Mullins, on the east bank of the River Barrow in Carlow; the river winds between high wooded banks, as it flows south

towards Waterford Harbour. We learn about Moling from a late Irish text transcribed in 1628 by Mícheál Ó Cléirigh, one of the compilers of the *Annals of the Four Masters*.[11]

Moling is said to have established a ferry across the River Barrow; it is still in existence. It is also claimed that he dug out a mile-long mill race to power the mill at St Mullins. His *Life* recounts that in 674 he secured from Finaghta, King of Meath, the remission of an annual cattle tribute (the *ború*), which had been exacted from the people of Leinster. Around 691, he became bishop of Ferns, which lies to the east, over the Blackstairs Mountains.

Chapel at St Mullins well, Carlow.

Moling's monastery

Early remains include the base of a round tower, a small chapel, 8ft long, and the remains of a high cross carved in granite in the ninth or tenth century, with a Crucifixion scene. On the opposite bank of the river is Moling's holy well: the water passes through a large pool into a well chapel, before flowing down to the River Barrow. In about 1160, Moling's monastery was annexed to the abbey of Augustinian canons at Ferns. The canons were responsible for building the six medieval churches, now in ruins, that dominate St Mullins; they may also have built St Moling's Mill.[12]

The Book of Mulling

There is a small, pocket-gospel book in Trinity College, Dublin, named the *Book of Mulling*; it is encased in an elaborate shrine of bronze with silver plates, and was probably written in the ninth century, copied from a manuscript written by Moling. It contains the gospels, with portraits of the evangelists, Matthew, Mark and John, and a Mass for the Sick, including the Creed.

The book also contains a simplified plan of the monastery at St Mullins, whose boundary wall is indicated by two concentric circles. Outside the enclosure, eight crosses commemorate Old Testament prophets and the four evangelists. One dedicated to the Holy Spirit was erected on or beside the boundary wall, and three more, possibly decorated with scenes from the scriptures, stood inside the compound. It is one of these three that survives at the site.

The plan suggests that monasteries were adorned with far more crosses than have survived, and the drawing provides unexpected evidence that crosses were erected outside the boundary wall of a monastic enclosure as well as within it. The fact that no buildings are marked on the plan, while the locations of the crosses are carefully plotted, also indicates that, symbolically at least, high crosses were a significant feature of Irish monastic life.

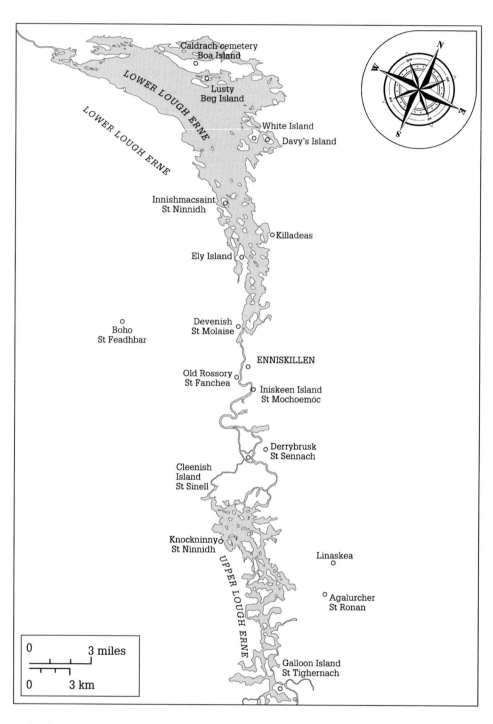

Early Christian sites around Lough Erne.

10

SAINTS OF LOUGH ERNE

I n early times there were no roads, so people often travelled by water; Ireland's many loughs were favourite places for monks to settle on islands or on their shores. As an example of this, we will examine the saints of Upper and Lower Lough Erne, which together form an inland waterway some 50 miles long. The lough is situated in Northern Ireland, near its western border, and extends through Cavan and Fernmanagh. Because the surrounding countryside was mainly bog and forest, the lough formed a natural highway. There are over 200 islands in Lough Erne, and some *crannogs* or artificial islands where homes were built on piles in early times. There is rich fishing in the lough for trout, pike, perch, rudd, bream and eels.

In about 837 the Vikings entered Donegal Bay, established a base at Belleek in the north-west, and plundered churches on the islands and shores of Lough Erne. The Normans failed to invade and colonise Fermanagh and Cavan, and so the area surrounding Lough Erne remained a conservative and independent region during the medieval period. At that time the Irish made no distinction between the Upper and Lower Lakes: Lough Erne was considered to extend from Belturbet in the south to the Falls of Assaroe beyond Belleek. The lough formed the main highway of Fermanagh until roads were constructed in the seventeenth century.

An isolated region

This area had always tended to be somewhat isolated. It was cut off from the seaport of Ballyshannon by the Assaroe Falls at the mouth of the Erne, and separated by mountains from easy access to much of the surrounding country. There are many small churches on islands or near the shore of the lough:

they suggest a picture of busy waterways, particularly on Sundays, and indicate the dependence of the population on water transport throughout medieval times. From the late twelfth century, some of the island churches maintained guest houses which accommodated pilgrims on their way to and from the pilgrimage centre of Lough Derg in Donegal.[1]

The absence of Norman settlement meant that the typical Norman parochial pattern, which consisted of building a church next to a castle in each small parish, was not introduced in the Lough Erne area. In Cavan and Fermanagh, parish churches were built on the same sites as early Christian churches, and were supported by the same monastic lands, administered by *erenaghs*.

In earlier times, the title *erenagh* usually referred to an abbot; by the medieval period, *erenaghs* were clerical families who provided food and services for the support of priests and bishops, and contributed to the upkeep of churches. The amount of church land farmed by *erenaghs* in Fermanagh during the medieval period was as much as one sixth of the county.[2] This suggests that the influence of the Church was quite strong in the region.

Devenish Island

This island is at the southern end of Lower Lough Erne, 3 miles north of Enniskillen; it has been uninhabited since 1922. Its name, *Daimhinis*, means 'Ox Island', which suggests that it offered good pasturage: it consists of about 123 acres of grazing land. In early Christian times, the monastery on Devenish Island was the most important in the lough: it became the centre of Fermanagh's cultural and spiritual life. At approximately the midpoint of the lough, Devenish was easily accessible by boat from both Upper and Lower Lough Erne.

A monastery was founded on Devenish in the sixth century by Molaise. A small twelfth-century oratory named after him may have been built over the first church on the island; it was roofed until the eighteenth century. What is said to have been the stone coffin of Molaise used to be in this chapel; it has now been moved to the Great Church. In about 650, Cuimin of Connor described Molaise's monastery of stone and recalled his hospitality:

> Molaise of the lake loved
> to live in a house of hard stone;
> strangers' home for the men of Erin,
> without refusal, without a sign of inhospitality.

The *Annals of Ulster*[3] state that Molaise died in both 563 and 570; his feast is 12 September. They also record that Devenish was attacked by Vikings in 837 and 923, noting that in 837 'all the Churches of Lough Erne, together with Cleenish and Devenish were destroyed by gentiles [Vikings]'. In 923 the *Annals* relate: 'a fleet of Foreigners on Lough Erne plundered the islands of the lake and the territories round it to and fro, and departed the following summer'. The monastery at Devenish was also burned in 1157.[4]

The *Céli Dé* (or Clients of God) may have lived here from early times; this monastic reform movement will be discussed more fully in Chapter 12. During the fifteenth and sixteenth centuries the *Céli Dé* of Devenish lived alongside the Augustinian community. By this time, the *Céli Dé* on the island had become secular non-monastic priests, and a residential annexe was built onto the original body of the church for them to live in. They served as parochial clergy and had a daughter church on the mainland, 4 miles downstream at Killadeas.

The round tower and Great Church

An impressive round tower, perhaps dating from the twelfth century, is perfectly preserved. It stands over 80ft high and tapers towards its conical cap. Hooks on its internal walls were possibly designed for hanging up leather satchels containing books or reliquaries. There is a doorway 9ft from the ground, and inside there are five storeys.

The base of a second round tower can be seen beside the present one; it was uncovered during excavation in 1973. This was either an earlier tower, or a false start, never completed. To the north-west of the round tower is a holy well; an ancient thorn tree formerly grew beside it. Some 130ft west of the tower are the remains of the Great Church (*Teampaill Mór*), also known as the Lower Church, dating from the thirteenth century; it served both the Celtic monks and the people of the parish of Devenish. Locals used the Lower Church until the late sixteenth century.[5]

Round tower and Lower Church, Devenish Island, Fermanagh.

The Great Church, Devenish Island, Fermanagh.

O'Dugan's cross, Devenish Island, Fermanagh.

St Mary's abbey

Higher up the hill are the ruins of St Mary's abbey. This was begun by the Augustinians in the twelfth century and reconstructed in the fifteenth and sixteenth centuries. There are remains of a guesthouse, refectory, chapter house and cloister to the north of the abbey. Nearby there is a fine cross, 6ft high, with an elaborately carved shaft and a crucifixion carved on its east face, dating from the fifteenth or sixteenth century. It was the work of a master mason called Matthew O'Dugan, and tells the story of creation. The difference in stone and finish between the cross head and its pillar suggest that they were not originally intended to form a single unit.

The hand bell and book shrine of Molaise

A small hand bell from Devenish is now in the National Museum, Dublin, and the shrine of Molaise can also be seen here. It was made to contain a copy of the gospels, but the manuscript has disappeared. The shrine is in the form of a small box made of bronze, covered with ornamental silver plates. On the front is a cross, with symbols of the four evangelists between its arms. An inscription at its base requests 'a prayer for Cennfailad, for the successor of Molaise, and for Gilla Baithin, the craftsman who carried out the embossment'. Cennfailad was Abbot of Devenish from 1001 to 1025; the craftsman had restored an earlier house-shaped shrine.

From May to September, there are boat trips in the afternoons from Brook Park, Enniskillen (on the A46 Belleek–Donegal road) offering a cruise of Lough Erne, which includes a visit to Devenish Island.

Killadeas

Killadeas is on the east shore of Lower Lough Erne, on the B82, north of Enniskillen. The ancient cemetery lies in the grounds of the late nineteenth-century Church of Ireland priory. The land was owned by the *Céli Dé* of Devenish: Killadeas, or *Cill Chéile Dé*, means 'church of the *Céli Dé*'. At some point it was known as the Yellow Church for, writing in 1644, Isaac Butler saw it on his way to Lough Derg and wrote: 'Two miles from Ballycassidy and ye ruins of ye Yellow Church on the roadside, it is rude sculpture and built like a barn.'[6]

There is an unusual group of carved stones in the cemetery, including a pillar stone, a holed stone, the so-called Bishop's Stone, and a multiple bullaun stone, which is a large pre-Christian standing stone with twelve cup-shaped hollows arranged in pairs. On the reverse side is carved a cross within a circle, with a long bifurcated stem. It was sketched by Macalister in 1949, who recorded an inscription to the left of the stem of the cross as: BENDACHT/ARART/ULUR/CAIN ('A blessing upon Art ua Lurcáin').[7] The inscription is no longer visible.

Bishop's Stone, Killadeas, Fermanagh.

The Bishop's Stone

The most remarkable sculpture at Killadeas has been named the Bishop's Stone; it was carved between the ninth and the twelfth century, two of its faces being worked at different times. On the narrow edge of the stone, the head of a youth is carved in high relief: he has rounded eyes, and a well-defined, slightly open mouth. Along his left eye and cheek are striating scars, perhaps acquired in battle. An interlace panel fills the space below.

A later sculptor altered the youth's face: part of his left cheek was cut off and straightened, in order to prepare the surface for carving the low relief figure of an elderly cleric on the adjacent side of the pillar.[8] This monk wears a short garment and pointed slippers; he holds a staff and a hand bell. His triangular head, elongated nose and chin, and his hunched back well convey the short, halting steps of an old cleric.

St Fanchea's monastery

Travelling south from Devenish, there are remains of two early monasteries. The first is on the western shore of Upper Lough Erne, on the south-western outskirts of Enniskillen, off the A509, in Old Rossory. A community was founded here by Fanchea, the sister of St Enda, in the late sixth century. She was said to be a native of Clogher, and to be buried at Killane. The monastery at Old Rossory was built on high ground overlooking the junction of the River Erne with the Upper Lough. Its cemetery can be seen on the edge of a housing estate.

Stories about Fanchea are recounted in the *Life of Enda*, whose conversion is said to have taken place at Old Rossory. While Enda was still a young warrior chieftain, he returned home, successful in battle, past Fanchea's monastery. He asked her for one of her young nuns in marriage, but the nun died and went to God, and Enda was guilt-stricken, and decided to become a monk. Since Fanchea's enclosure was unprotected, he dug a ditch round it and built a protecting rampart. Today, the rampart is still visible on the west side of the enclosure, 3ft high and 43ft wide. It must have been very impressive in medieval times, perhaps giving rise to this account of its construction.

Rampart, St Fanchea's monastery, Old Rossory, Fermanagh.

Cleenish Island

Some 5 miles south of Old Rossory, there was an early monastery on Cleenish Island in Upper Lough Erne, near Bellanaleck; it can be reached by a road bridge. This low-lying island is well described by its Gaelic name, *Cluan Innish*, or 'Meadow Island'. There is a chieftain's fort at the centre of the island, which has only one road, leading to an oval graveyard down by the lake shore, at the far end of the island. Sinell mac Mianaig, a monk known for his holiness and learning, and said to be a student of Finnian of Clonard, founded a monastery here in the sixth century. Columbanus studied here, according to the *Life of Columbanus* by Jonas of Bobbio, written in about 643.

Jonas relates that Columbanus was a handsome youth whom a woman hermit advised to flee the world. He did so against his mother's wishes, and studied under Abbot Sinell on Cleenish Island before moving to St Congall's monastery at Bangor, County Down, where he studied for many years before becoming a missionary. Jonas was an Italian monk who entered Bobbio in 618, only three years after the death of Columbanus; he wrote his *Life* using information from the immediate companions of Columbanus, so it is quite likely to be accurate.

Monastery graveyard, Cleenish Island, Fermanagh.

Cleenish cemetery

The *Annals of Ulster* describe a stone church built here in 1100, which was superseded by a medieval parish church. There are two early Christian cross slabs lying in the oval graveyard. A more elaborate cross slab from Cleenish is owned by Enniskillen Museum, but kept elsewhere. In 1790 the church and graveyard were despoiled of stones, headstones and monumental slabs, which were used to fill in the small arm of the lake where Enniskillen military barracks now stands.

Nevertheless, numerous stones from the medieval church survive at the site, many of them dressed, scattered about the graveyard. Significant among these is a decorative head of weathered sandstone, possibly the base of a gable coping, from an arch supporting the church roof. The face is peaceful, and its naturalistic features are finely carved; its curving hairline on both sides suggests wavy hair. About half of the top of the stone, immediately behind the head, has been carefully cut to form a shallow recess which may have held the angled stone of the gable.[9]

St Ninnidh

Another saint associated with Lough Erne is Ninnidh, whose nicknames were *leth derc* (meaning 'one-eyed') and *saobhruisc* ('squinting'). He was a sixth-century monk, said to have been born in Donegal, the grandson of the High King Laoire. Together with Molaise of Devenish, he is listed as one of the 'twelve apostles of Ireland' who trained under Finnian of Clonard. He appears to have evangelised Lough Erne, where both the parish of Knockninny in the Upper Lough and the island church of Inishmacsaint in the Lower Lough commemorate him.

Inishmacsaint

The name of this island means 'isle of the plain of sorrel'; as we saw in the previous chapter, this was valued as food in early times. There is a hill fort on the island, a high cross 14ft tall, and a fourteenth-century church built on early foundations, which was associated with Ninnidh. His hand bell was preserved on the island; it was said to have been given to him by St Senach of Derrybrusk, 12 miles to the south. The bell remained on Inishmacsaint until the mid-seventeenth century, and is now lost. An ancient overland route leads southwards via Glenwinney ('Ninnidh's glen') to Knockninny beside Upper Lough Erne, 18 miles to the south; it was perhaps used in rough weather when travel on the lough was difficult.[10]

Knockninny means 'Ninnidh's Hill'. At the foot of the hill, beside the lake shore, is Ninnidh's well; it is said to cure eye diseases. In 1739 it was described as

Ninnidh's well, Knockninny Quay, Upper Lough Erne, Fermanagh.

… a plentiful fountain of pure water, having a clearness and coolness scarce to be met with. It was at that time a popular spot for boatspeople to retire to for their entertainments, for which and around it are arranged benches of sod, and over it a shade of aquatic trees.[11]

Today shady trees still surround the well, and a modern equivalent has replaced the 'benches of sod'.

An early shrine

About 3 miles north-west of Inishmacsaint, an embanked enclosure at Abbey Point may indicate the site of an early monastery. Tully Castle was later erected on a hill overlooking the Point. In 1891, fishermen close to Abbey Point found an eighth-century bronze shrine, 24ft deep in the lough. The tomb-shaped shrine is rectangular with a sloping roof, and stands 6in high. It encloses a smaller tomb-shaped box which may have contained the relics of Ninnidh or some other local saint. The shrine is now in the National Museum of Ireland, Dublin.

Caldragh cemetery

Roughly 8 miles north of Inishmacsaint, there is a remarkable early cemetery on Boa Island at the northern end of Lower Lough Erne. Boa Island is now connected to the mainland by a causeway; when driving on A47 east from Belleek onto Boa Island, the cemetery is signed to the right. The island is named after the Celtic goddess of war, *Badhbha*. The oval cemetery contains a number of early, unmarked stones, and two remarkable figures, carved in early Christian times (*colour plate 16*).

It has been claimed that they represent pagan deities in a Christian society which still clung to pagan beliefs,[12] but it is more likely that they represent local monks. The oval cemetery is typical of a Christian settlement, and the lough was thoroughly Christianised by the time the two sculptures were created. Their style is not so different from the sculptures at Killadeas and on nearby White Island (see below), and it is unlikely that Christians would produce pagan idols on one island and Christian sculptures on another.

The smaller of the two figures was brought here in 1939; it was discovered on nearby Lusty Beg Island. The figure appears to be blind in one eye, and may depict the local saint, Ninnidh, who was nicknamed 'One-eyed', as we saw. The larger figure is 29in high and 18in wide; it depicts the upper torso of a double-sided figure. They have pear-shaped heads, and each has crossed arms and a belt; they share locks of braided hair. The lower half of the figure is broken off and lies alongside it, with large hands and long, straight fingers. There is a somewhat similar long-fingered figure carved in low relief in what may be an eighth-century context in the monastic cemetery at Carrowntemple in Sligo.[13]

*Double-faced figure,
Caldragh cemetery, Boa
Island, Lower Lough Erne,
Fermanagh.*

*Rear view of double-faced
figure with severed hand,
Caldragh cemetery, Boa
Island, Lower Lough Erne,
Fermanagh.*

White Island monastery

Around 4 miles south-east of Boa Island, two much smaller islands lie close to the eastern shore of the lough; both can be reached from the marina in the grounds of Castle Archdale, off the B82 on the east side of Lough Erne. There were monasteries on both Davy's Island and White Island, and on each there are remains of a twelfth-century church. That on White Island is near the landing stage; it was built around 1200, and contains an arched Romanesque doorway (*colour plate 17*). It is enclosed by a stone wall, and is built on the site of an earlier monastery, surrounded by an embankment.

In 1958, figures from the early church on White Island were found, carved in quartzite, probably dating from the ninth or tenth centuries; they had been used as building stones in the later church. Since the *Annals of Ulster* record that Vikings attacked and destroyed the monasteries in Lough Erne in about 837, these carvings may have lain in the ruins of the first church for four hundred years before they were incorporated into the Romanesque church. This unique group of eight carved stones is now secured to the north side of the south wall of the later church.

The carved figures

The sculptures are strongly characterised and of a high quality. It has been suggested that because of the sockets on top of their heads, six of the statues may have supported a pulpit or preaching chair of an earlier, possibly wooden,

church. They appear to form three pairs of caryatids, each pair being of a different height.[14] An unfinished, roughly blocked-out figure, now secured to the north wall to the right of the three pairs, indicates that the sculptures were carved here on the island.

One of the tallest statues depicts an abbot, wearing a hemmed tunic, holding a bell and a crook; it might be a portrait of the abbot of the monastery. The second carving of the pair is a more symbolic sculpture which may represent King David as shepherd and psalmist. A pouch hangs from his belt; one hand is held up to his mouth and the other holds a scroll. The scroll could represent a psalter, from which

Abbot, with bell and crook, White Island, Lower Lough Erne, Fermanagh.

Seven figures, White Island, Lower Lough Erne, Fermanagh.

David sings the psalms which he has composed. As a young shepherd, David carried sling stones in a pouch, in order to kill wild animals and, later, Goliath (1 Samuel 17. 40).

The middle pair of statues might depict Christ or King David. One holds a pair of animals, while the other is a warrior clasping a small circular shield over a short sword; he wears a penannular brooch. The smallest pair of figures includes a *Sheela na Gig* and a small seated figure holding a long rectangular object, perhaps a book. This may represent Christ, since it resembles a seated Christ in the *Book of Kells*. The *Sheela na Gig* is a cross-legged female figure wearing a cape, with a grinning face and puffy cheeks; her hands rest on her thighs. She is a magical figure often found over church windows and door-ways, who perhaps represents lust, a temptation to be avoided by monks.

Galloon Island

Situated 40 miles south of White Island, at the southern end of Upper Lough Erne, Galloon Island is the site of the first monastery founded by St Tighernach, (or Tiernan), a sixth-century monk. He was one of the chief saints of the territory ruled by the Uí Chremthainn dynasty, together with Mac Caírthinn of Clogher (see Chapter 2) and Molaise of Devenish. Two shafts of high crosses survive in the monastery graveyard on the island. According to his Latin *Life*, he offered Galloon to Congall of Bangor before moving 9 miles east to Clones.

Clones Abbey

The town of Clones in Monaghan was formerly almost surrounded by water. Here, Tighernach is said to have lived as a hermit, until he died of plague in about 550; his feast day is 4 April. The earliest surviving feature of the monastic site is a tenth-century round tower, one of the earliest in Ireland; its base shows evidence of attempts to destroy it by fire. A short distance away, in the centre of the town, is a fine high cross; its head and shaft may have come from two separate tenth-century crosses. Its carved images include Adam and Eve, Abraham sacrificing Isaac, and Daniel in the lions' den; on the opposite side are scenes from the New Testament.

Tighernach's Shrine

Near the round tower in the abbey graveyard is a stone shrine, shaped like a church, with a worn carving of a bishop at one end. It is known as St Tighernach's Shrine (*colour plate 18*), and was originally made to contain a relic, possibly of Tighernach; it was probably erected in the twelfth century, and placed near the high altar of the great church of Clones, which was demolished during the Nine Years' War (1688–97). The shrine is carved from a single block of sandstone, and represents an early Christian church.[15]

Clones abbey was destroyed by fire in 835, 1095 and 1164. The monks at Clones adopted the Rule of Augustine several decades before the Anglo-Norman invasion in the twelfth century. In 1207 Hugh de Lacy destroyed the abbey and town, but five years later they were rebuilt by the English, who also erected a castle here. The Reformation led to the suppression of the monasteries by Henry VIII in the sixteenth century, and that of Clones was destroyed. By the seventeenth century it was a ruin, but solitary monks continued to live in the locality until the eighteenth century. An English garrison was later established within the ruins.[16]

Other monks of Upper Lough Erne

Lough Erne was the home to many groups of monks in early times. Among others, St Mochoemóc lived on Iniskeen Island in the sixth or seventh century, near Cleenish Island; there is a church here and the shaft of a high cross. In the hills 8 miles to the north-west, the author of the *Martyrology of Óengus*, writing in the first part of the ninth century, relates that St Feadhbar (or Faber) lived at Boho, where there is a fine tenth-century high cross in the Catholic church of Toneel North.

Located 4 miles to the east of Upper Lough Erne, Lisnaskea was probably the tribal headquarters of a small kingdom named *Fir Manach*, meaning 'The men of Manach'. This group came from Leinster, and were named after an ancestor, Monach; they gave their name to County Fermanagh. The shaft of a high cross stands in the old Potato Market at the centre of the town; it came from a nearby monastery whose site is unknown.

Some 2 miles east of the lough, between Lisnaskea and Galloon Island, Agalurcher is the site of another early monastery. It is associated with a seventh-century monk named Ronan, of the royal family of Airgialla. Early calendars list his festival as 23 December and also associate another more obscure saint with the site. By medieval times, this was an important parish church. In fifteenth- and early sixteenth-century annals we hear of men killed at the altar and at the gate and taken prisoner here – all probably violations of sanctuary. Part of a medieval building survives at the site, while a twelfth-century carving of a mitred bishop bearing a book and crosier may belong to the tomb shrine of St Ronan; it is now in Fermanagh County Museum in Castle Enniskillen.[17]

Because of the isolation of this region until relatively recently, Upper and Lower Lough Erne, together with their hinterlands, afford us a unique glimpse of life in early Christian times, with many island sites, a variety of monastic remains, and a strong sculptural tradition. Nevertheless, Ireland is a country bisected by loughs, and each of these waterways has its own early Christian story to tell.

11

IRISH MISSIONARIES

There were some remarkable Irish missionaries, including Columbanus, Fursa and Kilian, but 'mission' was rarely their primary aim. Most of them preferred to describe themselves as *peregrini*, or 'strangers'. This was a difficult act of exile: criminals were sent overseas as a punishment, but monks chose their exile. Their outer journey enabled them to make an inner journey of detachment from all they held dear. Those who went abroad often found themselves in the service of kings, who wanted them to go into hostile areas and convert pagans; thus they became missionaries almost by chance.

Peregrini: strangers

In early Irish law, the *tuath*, or provincial kingdom, was seen as an extended tribal family, within which one found protection. Those who left home divested themselves of their rights. Those who left the tribe to marry outside it were considered to be of little value: a man who 'followed his wife's buttocks' over the border of his *tuath* had fewer rights than his wife. Jesus offered a model of leaving his house and family, and monks chose a similar penance; *peregrini* were described as flotsam and jetsam thrown up by the sea (*muircorthe*).[1]

A number of seventh-century *peregrini* arrived at the frontier of what is now Germany, where they lived among either pagans or heretics. Columbanus founded a community in Lombardy in northern Italy among Arian heretics. Once settled, a monk would establish a monastery with his followers, which was a place of retreat, situated between the secular and the sacred, between slavery in the Egypt of this world and the Promised Land of heaven. Holiness radiates outwards from a monastery, and *peregrini* became missionaries by living a holy life.

Searching for a desert

Eucherius of Lyons (d. *c.* 449) wrote homilies and letters which were widely read in monasteries, including a letter entitled 'In praise of the desert' (*de laudi heremi*).[2] After the death of his wife, Eucherius retired to the island monastery of Lérins, between Marseilles and Nice; he was appointed bishop of Lyons in 434. Both his sons became monks of Lérins, and then bishops. Eucherius had experience of marriage and of monastic life; he understood the service of God both outside and inside a monastery. For him, life in the desert of the monastery was focussed on the Promised Land of heaven.

A desert was primarily an empty place, a place of retreat. Some *peregrini* travelled north in search of their monastic desert. Irish monks sailed with the Norse to Iceland, and after the seventh century, Anglo-Saxon monks joined them. Iceland was officially pagan, but many Irish Christians lived there, as we can tell from Irish place names and Christian inhumations in cemeteries. It is estimated that 43 per cent of the population of Iceland during the period 870–930 were genetically Irish.[3]

Willibrord (658–739) was an Anglo-Saxon from Northumbria, who lived in Ireland for twenty years, and then travelled to Europe, where he worked in Holland, Luxembourg, Germany and Frisia in the 700s. The French monk Ansgar (801–65) preached in Germany, Denmark and Sweden. Both men probably brought Irish monks with them: there are Irish crosiers and other Christian objects in Scandinavia, not pillaged by Norsemen but brought there by ninth- and tenth-century missionary monks.[4]

The desert in the ocean

There were no deserts in Europe, but the waters lying off the north and west coasts of Scotland were seen as the next best thing by Irish monks. As the ancient Israelite slaves journeyed through the desert to the Promised Land, monks believed that by sailing across the watery desert they would reach the Promised Land of heaven at the far edge of the world. According to Adomnán's *Life of Columba*, on the edge of the Ardnamurchan peninsula, north of Mull, was 'the great sea bag [or 'bay'] of paradise': a place at the westernmost end of the Scottish peninsula, at the furthest end of the earth, from which monks could view paradise. They held similar beliefs about the westernmost points of

Ireland, where the cults of Patrick and Columba were strong: Patrick took the gospel as far as Mayo in the west, and Brendan's friend, Barrind set out for the Promised Land from Teelin Bay at the foot of Slieve League on the west coast of Donegal.[5]

The phrase 'desert in the ocean' (*desertum in oceano*) is found only in Adomnán's *Life of Columba*. He uses it three times, two of which describe the various journeys of Cormac, who searches for an ocean hermitage. The first time, Cormac sets out from Mayo, but fails to reach his 'desert' because he travels with a monk who had no permission from his abbot to do so:

> ... Saint Columba prophesied as follows concerning Cormac, grandson of Lethan, a holy man, who on no less than three occasions toiled in search of a desert hermitage in the ocean, but without finding one. 'Once again today', he said, 'Cormac sets sail in search of a desert hermitage ... But not even on this occasion will he find what he seeks, and for no other fault of his, but that he has wrongly taken with him as companion on the voyage a monk of a devout abbot, who departed without the abbot's permission.[6]

Later, Cormac set sail from Iona in search of a desert in the ocean, with Columba's blessing, and reached an island beyond Orkney. He returned safely, after Columba interceded on his behalf with Brude, King of the Picts, to grant him a safe passage. Cormac later set out on a final voyage, beyond the realms of human knowledge: a south wind drove him northwards for two weeks, where his curragh was attacked by stinging creatures, perhaps jellyfish, which threatened to penetrate his boat of skins. Its leather hide is understood as a symbol of our fragile flesh. Adomnán relates that Columba and his monks prayed fervently to God, who sent a north wind, which blew Cormac safely home.[7]

There was no guarantee that a monk might reach a desert in the ocean, especially if it was one's own idea in the first place. In another account Adomnán describes a monk's unsuccessful search for a hermitage in the ocean. Baitan asks Columba to bless his quest, but the abbot foretells that it will fail:

> ... A certain Baitan, of the race of nia-Taloirc, asked to be blessed by the saint before going to search with others for a desert hermitage in the sea. Bidding him farewell, the saint uttered this prophecy concerning him: 'This man, who is going to search for a desert hermitage in the ocean, will not lie at rest in a desert place, but will be buried in that place where a woman will drive sheep across his grave.'[8]

This ultimate indignity happened after Baitan returned home to Ireland, and was buried in the oak woods of Derry.

Columbanus

Chief among the Irish missionaries to Europe was Columbanus (543–615). Unusually, a considerable number of his own works survive, including letters and sermons, monastic Rules and possible poems; we therefore know a great deal about Columbanus, his passionate love of God and his ascetic ideals. He believed that his vocation was to renounce security and shelter, and so obey Christ's command to leave father and mother for the sake of the kingdom of God (Mt. 10. 37; Mk. 10. 7). In his third sermon, Columbanus wrote: 'We want to persist in living on the road as wanderers, as aliens, as strangers on earth.'

The *Life of Columbanus* by a monk of Bobbio named Jonas was written in about 643, only thirty years after the death of Columbanus in that community. According to convention, the *Life* is primarily concerned with miracles and other traditional hagiograpical material, including cures, answers to prayer, the saint's second sight, and his power over animals. Nevertheless, we are also told some facts.

Jonas relates that Columbanus was born in Leinster of a noble family, and was well educated. As we saw in the previous chapter, he began his monastic life on Cleenish Island in Upper Lough Erne, under the direction of St Sinell. He later joined Congall's monastery of Bangor at the head of Belfast Lough in north-east Ireland until he was about thirty, when he sailed to Gaul with twelve companions. He worked in Merovingian Gaul for over twenty years, before spending the last few years of his life in northern Italy. Because of his example, his inspiration and his pioneering achievements, Columbanus is considered to be the greatest of Ireland's missionaries to Europe.

Columbanus arrives in Europe

The group of monks are said to have landed in Brittany, east of St Malo, at Plage Duguesclin. According to local Breton traditions, he first stayed on a tiny wooded island in the bay (*colour plate 19*); the later parish church of Saint-Coulomb was built nearby. The church was rebuilt in the nineteenth century; its tower dates from 1778 (see photo overleaf). Columbanus is popular in Brittany, where eleven parishes are named after him.[9]

The monks continued on foot to Luxeuil in the Vosges mountains, where King Childebert of Austrasia gave Columbanus a ruined Roman fort for a monastery at Annegray. The community grew, and Columbanus then established Fontaines and Luxeuil, which became one of the leading monasteries in Europe, sending monks as far as Bavaria. They lived according to Irish traditions, keeping the Irish date of Easter, and observing Irish penitential practice, with a bishop who was subordinate to the abbot. These differences from the Frankish Church created friction with the local clergy, particularly over the celebration of Easter.

Saint-Coulomb church, Cancale, Brittany.

Columbanus therefore wrote to Pope Gregory the Great affirming his loyalty to Rome, but claiming that the Irish calendar was that of the earliest Christians. A few years later, when attacked by the archbishop of Lyons, he wrote to the Synod of Chalons, asking them to allow his communities to follow Irish customs. Columbanus was invited by King Theodoric II to the Burgundy court, where he refused to bless the illegitimate sons of the new king, disregarding the opposition of Queen Brunehaut. She had him expelled, and the monks sailed down the Loire to the sea, under military escort, to be deported to Ireland, but conditions were unfavourable for sailing, so the monks returned to Nantes, and began preaching in the region.

St Gall, Switzerland

Columbanus then went to the court of King Clothair II of Neustria and later to Metz where, at King Theudebert's court, he met some of his monks from Luxeuil. From there, they rowed up the Rhine, hoping to settle at Bregenz on Lake Constance. After again encountering opposition, Columbanus decided to cross the Alps into Italy. His companion Gall (d. *c.* 630), who had come from Bangor with him, remained in Switzerland, living as a hermit. A century later a community was established on the site of Gall's hermitage, and the town of St Gall grew around it. In about 613 Columbanus settled at Bobbio in northern Italy, where he and his followers built a monastery on the site of a ruined church. He died two years later aged about seventy-two; he was buried in Bobbio, while his pastoral staff was taken back across the Alps to his friend Gall in Switzerland.

Many Irishmen joined the monastery of St Gall, and it accumulated a priceless collection of early manuscripts. Some have Irish poetry written in the margins, like this poem from a ninth-century grammar book of Priscian:

A hedge of trees surrounds me, a blackbird's lay sings to me, praise I shall not
    conceal,
Above my lined book the trilling of the birds sings to me,
A clear-voiced cuckoo sings to me in a grey cloak from the tops of bushes,
May the Lord save me from Judgement; well do I write under the greenwood.[10]

In Irish thought, the interpretation of birdsong was an aspect of the diviner's
craft; like druids before them, true monks were considered able to understand
the language of birds.

Writings of Columbanus

Many of the writings of Columbanus have been lost, but what survives dem-
onstrates his classical training: he was familiar with Horace and quotes Virgil
extensively. He also refers to Juvenal, Martial and Salust, although it is thought
that he may have received these texts through the works of Christian scholars.
His guidelines for monks include two Rules and a Penitential. The *Penitential
of Columbanus* draws on that of Finnian of Clonard, and on Cassian's medical
theory of curing by opposites; it focuses on sin as a sickness in need of healing.
The Penitential is divided into three parts: first, sins of monks; secondly, sins
of secular clergy and thirdly, the sins of lay people. It was probably composed
when Columbanus was in Europe, where it was widely used.

Rules for monks

Columbanus was formed by monastic life in Bangor, where he had been
trained. His two Rule books, *Regula Monachorum* and *Regula Cenobialis*
(cenobites being monks who lived in community), provide more detailed commentaries on monastic life than any other Irish source. In these two Rules he
stresses unquestioning obedience and rigorous asceticism; unlike his other
writings, they are simple in both content and style. They set out what is to
be expected of monks although, in contrast to later Rules, such as that of
Benedict of Nursia, the abbot's role is not described.

    Columbanus required monks to perform the Office which Cassian recom-
mended: this mainly consisted of psalms, and was less elaborate than others
used on mainland Europe at the time. He prescribed three psalms for each
daytime 'Hour' and a lengthy, though variable, Night Office. This appears to
have consisted of twelve psalms at dusk, twelve at midnight and a complex
Dawn service. As the nights lengthened in autumn, the number of psalms
increased, until seventy-five were chanted nightly. They then appear to have
decreased by three per week until the short summer nights, when only thirty-
six were sung. At the same time, there would have been more manual work in
the longer summer days, harvesting crops.

Early copy of the Rule for Monks *of Columbanus (Bib. Nat. Ms. Lat. 6333), Landévennec, Finistère, Brittany.*

The *Rule for Monks* addresses the first principles of monastic life, rather than its daily details; it is quite severe. It includes ten chapters, on obedience, silence, food and drink, poverty, vanity, chastity, the Office in choir, discernment, mortification and perfection. The final chapter describes the perfect monk:

> Let the monk live in a community under the discipline of one father and in company with many, so that from one he may learn lowliness, from another patience. For one may teach him silence and another meekness. Let him not do as he wishes, let him eat what he is bidden, ... be subject to whom he does not like. Let him come weary to bed and sleep walking, and let him be forced to rise while his sleep is not yet finished. Let him keep silence when he has suffered wrong, let him fear the superior of the community as a lord, love him as a father ...[11]

Letters and poems

Six of the Letters of Columbanus survive: they are studied and exhortatory in tone. The first was written to Pope Gregory the Great, in about 600, insisting on the superiority of the Irish calendar, as we saw. His letter of 603 is addressed to the French bishops, declining to attend the Synod of Chalons, to which he had been summoned. The letters seem deliberately intellectual, employing a complex word order, figures of speech such as puns, and words with Greek derivations. His last letter is entitled 'To a young follower': we do not know who this was.

It is possible that five of the six poems attributed to Columbanus are genuine. Their subject is the brevity of human life. One is dedicated to Hunaldo, who was perhaps a pupil; it is written as an acrostic poem with his name and Hunaldo's forming the first letter of each line. Another short poem, 'To Fidolio', concerns the evils of wealth; it is illustrated by many classical allusions.

Sermons of Columbanus

Thirteen sermons survive, preached in Milan in 613, during his old age; they are the finest sermons from the Irish Church of this period. Milan was the capital of Lombardy, where the Arian heresy was strong. Arians disputed the traditional theology of the Trinity, which may account for a Trinitarian emphasis in his sermons. They reveal Columbanus as a theologian and teacher with a deep understanding of the meaning of life and a passionate love of God. In sermon twelve he preaches: 'Let us love you [Christ], love only you, yearn only for you, think only of you, day and night, so that your love occupies our whole mind and soul'.

In sermons five and eight he reflects that human life is only a pathway to our spiritual homeland in heaven. Sermon eleven contains advice on life in community, and describes the spiritual training of the monastic vocation. Sermon thirteen is a beautiful reflection on the Eucharist, in which his listeners are invited to slake their thirst at the fountain of living water which Christ offers (Jn. 4. 14). In passionate poetry, he prays:

> ... Admit me to that fountain, merciful God, righteous Lord, so that there I too might drink of the living water and, ravished by his too great loveliness, might hold to him always on high and say: How lovely is the fount of living water, whose water does not fail, springing up to life eternal ... Give us this water always, Lord Christ, that it may be in us too a fountain of water that lives and springs up to eternal life. I ask for great things; who does not know that. But you, King of Glory, know how to give great things ...[12]

Dedications in England

Unlike most Irish saints, Columbanus has almost no dedications in Ireland or England. In this he might be considered a true *peregrinus*, or stranger, who lived outside his homeland. It is possible that the Cornish churches St Columb Major and St Columb Minor (5 and 2 miles east of Newquay respectively), are dedicated to Columbanus: his monks could have made the overland crossing back and forth from Ireland to Gaul near to St Columb Major, which became one of the wealthiest churches in Cornwall. However, no documents survive relating to these churches before the thirteenth century, and a late sixteenth-century poem in Cornish describes Columb as a foreign princess who was pursued and murdered by a tyrant.[13]

The only undisputed English dedication to Columbanus is the chapel of the Saxon palace at Cheddar in Somerset, where the Kings of Wessex Community School now stands on the site of an early medieval settlement, and possibly a Celtic one.[14] In 1960 Philip Rahtz discovered the remains of an Anglo-Saxon palace in the grounds of the school. The building was made of wood, and had a thatched roof. This first timber hall was dated to the late-ninth century, to the very end of King Alfred's reign. According to the *Anglo-Saxon Chronicle*, the Kings of Wessex met here in 942, 956 and 968. The site can be visited: outlined in the grass are the positions of a twelfth- to fourteenth-century great hall and a twelfth-century *witan*, or council chamber.

There are substantial remains of a tenth-century chapel dedicated to Columbanus (*colour plate 20*): the discovery of a single tenth-century coin helped to date the building. The chapel's dedication may be explained by intermarriage between the Saxon royal family and that of Lotharingia, a region which is now split between eastern France and western Germany; this was an area where Columbanus had worked. In the eleventh century, one of the bishops of Wells came from Lotharingia. The chapel was rebuilt in the eleventh century and again in the thirteenth, when the bishops of Wells restored both the chapel and the east hall. By now, the complex was probably no more than a royal hunting lodge with a hall, a chapel and a domestic annexe.[15]

The impact of Columbanus

Followers of Columbanus established monasteries on mainland Europe at Faremoutiers (627), Jouarre (630) and Rebais (636), and large numbers of Irish monks travelled to Europe over the next two centuries. Some found leading positions at the court of the Emperor Charlemagne at Aachen; others travelled as far as Taranto in southern Italy and Kiev in Russia. Gradually, European monasteries replaced the *Rule of Columbanus* with that of the Italian-born Benedict, but medieval Christian Europe was to a great extent shaped by the Irish, and in particular, by Columbanus and his followers.

Kilian

Compared with Columbanus, Kilian is a more shadowy figure: none of his writings survive, but a *Vita* was written at the monastery of Fulda in the last quarter of the tenth century, and there are two earlier *Passiones*, or accounts of his sufferings. These are stereotyped, and deliberately set in an old-fashioned mode: in the eighth century, a *Passio* was considered more appropriate than a miracle-filled *Vita*, since Kilian was honoured as a martyr. Kilian (*c.* 640– *c.* 689) was born a hundred years after Columbanus. Unlike Columbanus, however, Kilian is revered in his tribal territory in Ireland. His name means 'one who lives in a cell, or hermitage'.

Mullagh

Kilian is said to have been born in Mullagh, 8 miles north of Kells in Cavan, into the Cailenga family, who ruled eastern Cavan and northern Meath. Kilian and his companions may have trained as monks at Ros Alithir monastery (now Ross Carbery) in County Cork. There is a possible dedication to Kilian at Kilmachillogue, near Kenmare in Kerry. From here he is said to have left Ireland to go on pilgrimage to Europe in 680; he evangelised Franconia and was martyred there at the age of about fifty; his feast is 8 July. In 1991, a relic of Kilian was brought back from Würzburg to Mullagh, where it can be seen in the Catholic church. Across the road, the St Kilian Heritage Centre contains an excellent display of information and facsimiles of early manuscripts.

Mullagh is an early Christian site, although it would have been associated with Kilian only after his death, when his cult developed some centuries later. In the cemetery beside Lough Mullagh, an ogham-inscribed stone was found, dating from before the eighth century. The letters on it have been deciphered as OSBAR, possibly a Saxon name, but the upper part of the stone may be missing. Nearby in the lake, a *crannog* is the site of a local chieftain's dwelling. Kilian's holy well is a mile west of Mullagh on the road to Virginia, just before the only bridge, at a bend in the road, to the left. A pattern was celebrated here in Kilian's honour until the early nineteenth century.

Crannog in Lough Mullagh, Cavan.

Kilian's holy well, Mullagh, Cavan.

Kilian in Franconia

According to Kilian's *Passio*, he set sail for Europe with eleven companions. They journeyed along the Rhine and the Maine into Franconia. Together with two companions, a priest named Colonat (or Colmán) and a deacon named Totnan, and with the pope's permission, Kilian converted the Franconian ruler, Duke Gosbert. His other nine companions evangelised other regions. Duke Gosbert was married to his brother's wife, Geilana, and Kilian ordered him to leave her. Geilana was furious, and had Kilian executed together with his two companions. However, the executioner killed himself, and Geilana was tormented by an evil spirit until she too died. The story is modelled on that of John the Baptist who denounced Herod for living with his brother's wife, and the subsequent murder of John on the orders of Herodias, Herod's new wife (Mt. 14. 3-12).

Veneration of Kilian

Around 752, the remains of the three Irishmen were discovered buried in a stable. They were disinterred and buried in a round church on the Marienburg. Soon, pilgrims flocked to the shrine, including many from Ireland. In 1139 the Schottenkloster of St James, an Irish monastery in Würzburg, was founded to accommodate Irish pilgrims; it survived for 350 years. For a time it maintained a daughter house in Ross Carbery, in west Cork. The cult of Kilian has remained strong in Germany; the Kilianfest of Würzburg is still an important festival. Medieval hymns were composed in Latin and German to honour Kilian, and he was depicted on seals and coins in the Würzburg region.

An Irish manuscript survives of St Paul's Letters, created in the second half of the eighth century; it is now in the University Library, Würzburg. This manuscript is an important text for research into Old Irish; it probably came to Würzburg within the context of veneration of Kilian in the ninth century. The Latin text is written in Irish minuscule; the initials are accentuated by red and yellow. The codex was given Latin and Old Irish glosses while still in Ireland; it illustrates the deep preoccupation of Irish monks with the scriptures. It may have been brought to Würzburg by the Irishman Clemens Scottus when he travelled to Kilian's grave in 826, wishing to die there.[16]

Early accounts of Kilian

The oldest texts which refer to Kilian are an eighth-century necrology at Würzburg and an entry by Hrabanus Maurus (*c.* 780–856), abbot of Fulda and archbishop of Mainz, in his *Martyrology*. The early accounts of Kilian state that his relics were recovered intact from his grave after his martyrdom, together with his Gospel book, a manuscript produced in France around 600. In about 1090, the book was rebound in Bamberg, and an ivory relief was created to form its cover. The relief is 10in by 7in, and depicts the decapitation of Kilian and his companions in front of an acanthus tree and a vine, to symbolise the

Ivory cover of Kilian's Gospel book: replica at Mullagh, Cavan.

Eucharist and the cross, realities held dear by the three martyrs. Above this scene, angels bear their souls to heaven in a cloth.[17]

The story of the life and martyrdom of Kilian is first found in the *Passio Minor*, the shortest description of Kilian's life, which was probably written at the beginning of the ninth century, when Kilian was venerated as an imperial Carolingian saint, about a generation after his relics had been discovered. The oldest sequence of illustrations of his life is a series of eleven miniatures in the tenth-century *Vita* composed at Fulda. Its text corresponds to the *Passio Minor*; it is preserved in the Lower Saxon District Library, Hanover (Ms.L.189). The miniatures are incorporated into the text; they are likely to be the earliest detailed illustrations of any saint's life. The miniature in the photograph opposite is painted in opaque colours on a mauve background.

Kilian is received by Duke Gosbert. Miniature from Kilian's Vita, *Fulda.*

The two Carolingian *Passiones* recount the life and death of Kilian. It was previously thought that these two accounts dated from the tenth or eleventh centuries, but they are now considered to be earlier. The shorter one must have been created in Würzburg between 750 and 840 at the latest, while the longer account was probably composed later, under Bishop Gozbald (842–55).[18] The *Passiones* were designed to keep Kilian's memory alive: the value of the two works lies not in their historical accuracy but in their depiction of an early medieval world view and mentality, with their purpose of presenting Kilian as an exemplary witness to the faith, and as a model of devotion to Christ and his Church.

12

MÁELRÚAIN AND THE CLIENTS OF GOD

By the eighth century, communities varied widely in their worship and practice, and there was a desire to return to the ascetic holiness of early monastic life. A leading figure in this movement was Máelrúain (d. 792), who founded a monastery at Tallaght, now a southern suburb of Dublin, on land given to him by the King of Leinster in 774. In early times, Tallaght was a remote region at the foot of the mountains; a church was built on the site of the monastery in 1829, partly from medieval remains. Another prominent figure was Dublittir of Finglas (d. 796), whose community was also in County Dublin. The monks became known as *Céli Dé*, meaning 'Clients (or Servants) of God'. They also described themselves as 'true clerics' (*fírcléirigh*), 'sons of life' (*mac bethad*) or 'clerics in the South' (*cléirich ind deiscirt*), since they originated in Munster.[1]

The movement spread from Munster to other parts of Ireland, and as far as Iona. Its leaders were highly respected: Dublittir presided over the clergy at an assembly in Tara. The monasteries of Tallaght and Finglas were called 'the two eyes of Ireland', and the most important writings of the *Céli Dé* originated from them. Dublittir's way of life was more flexible than that of Máelrúain, who was critical of his monastic neighbour. Both placed great emphasis on individual holiness: Dublittir recited the 150 psalms standing, prostrating himself after each psalm.[2]

Máelrúain

Little is known of Máelrúain's life, but a number of writings originate from him: *The Teaching of Máelrúain* (*Teagasg Máelrúain*), the *Rule of the Céli Dé*, and *The Monastery of Tallaght*. Máelrúain's *Rule* was severe: monks should stay in their monasteries continuously, instead of going into exile for the love of God, as the *peregrini* did. He insisted on the primacy of communal prayer, with its repetition of psalms and genuflections. Máelrúain required poverty, chastity and obedience, although other teachers emphasised a monk's voluntary submission, rather than blind obedience.

Sundays were observed as strictly as the Jewish Sabbath, when no work could be done. Lengthy prayer vigils were encouraged, sometimes standing with arms outstretched in the form of a cross. However, extreme asceticism was discouraged, in order to avoid both gossip and pride. Mac Oige of Lismore (d. 753) praised normality, commenting 'Never was it said: this man is too steady'. Máelrúain taught that monks were entitled to collect tithes, a tenth of the produce of everyone else, and encouraged conformity to Roman practices.

During communal meals the gospels were read, one during each of the seasons, and the monks were questioned about the reading, since understanding the scriptures was considered important. Study and labour were significant features of the monastic day. Máelrúain wrote:

> [There are] three profitable things in the day: prayer, labour and study, or it may be teaching or writing or sewing clothes, or any profitable work that a monk may do, so that none may be idle … Labour in piety is the most excellent work of all. The kingdom of heaven is granted to him who directs study, him who studies and him who supports the student.

Máelrúain wrote of the temptation that women posed to monks, and insisted on celibacy, for both monks and other clerics. He emphasised spiritual direction and the confession of sin. Each monk was to have a spiritual father or soul-friend (*anmchara*), to whom faults were to be confessed immediately, and not withheld until the end of the week. Devotion to Our Lady and to the Archangel Michael, the traditional guardian against evil, was encouraged.

There was a strong emphasis on liturgy and on imitating the saints who had preceded them. In order to foster their cults, martyrologies, or calendars of saints and their feast days, were compiled. The *Martyrology of Tallaght* probably originated on Lindisfarne, and passed through Iona and Bangor in Ireland, where Irish scribes made additions to the text. It then reached Tallaght, where most of its Irish additions were made, probably by Óengus the Culdee, after he had completed the *Martyrology of Óengus* (or *Félire Óengusso*).

Óengus

The only sources of information about Óengus the Culdee are internal evidence from the *Félire*, a later, Middle-Irish preface to the *Félire*, the entry for his feast day inserted into the *Martyrology of Tallaght*, and a biographical poem. According to the Middle-Irish preface, he was born of a royal Ulster family, and educated at the monastery of Clonenagh, near present-day Moutrath in Laois. He lived as a hermit at *Díseart Beitheach* (or 'Birch Tree Desert'), where he followed an austere lifestyle. Óengus later joined the community at Tallaght, concealing his identity and his learning, and was given menial tasks, until he coached an unsuccessful student, and his wisdom became evident.

Máelrúain is described as the mentor or foster father (*aite*) of Óengus, who later returned to Clonenagh, where he died in old age, perhaps in the mid-ninth century. However, his association with Clonenagh may have been a later invention, since the *Félire* gives no such importance to Clonenagh. A list of saints inserted into the *Martyrology of Tallaght* describes Óengus as a bishop; if so, his influence may have extended to the reformed communities associated with Tallaght, many of which were founded during the lifetime of Óengus. Two such monasteries in Limerick and Laois, both called *Díseart Óengussa* (Óengus's Hermitage), are named after him.

The Martyrology of Óengus

The *Félire Óengusso* is the earliest metrical martyrology to be written in the vernacular. It survives in at least ten manuscripts, the earliest being the *Leabhar Breac*, dating from the early fifteenth century. It includes a long prologue and epilogue, and many poems. Later scribes inserted a prose preface, including material on Óengus, and added many glosses to the text. A poem preserved in the *Leabhar Breac*, composed in the late ninth century by a monk also named Óengus, recalls how his master lived, beside the 'cold, pure' river:

> Delightful to sit here thus
> By the side of the cold pure Nore:
> Though it was frequented, it was never a path of raids
> In glorious Birch Tree Desert.
>
> Birch Tree Desert where dwelt the man
> Whom hosts of angels were wont to visit;
> A pious cloister behind a circle of crosses,
> Where Óengus Mac Uibhlinne used to be.
>
> Óengus from the assembly of heaven,
> Here are his tomb and his grave;
> 'Tis hence he went to death
> On a Friday to holy heaven.
>
> 'Tis in Clonenagh he was reared,
> In Clonenagh he was buried;
> In Clonenagh of many crosses
> He first read his psalms.[3]

Other writings of the *Céli Dé*

The *Stowe Missal* was written soon after Máelrúain's death, probably at Terryglass in Tipperary; it is a unique record of the Irish liturgy.[4] The manuscript is a sacramentary, or guide for administering sacraments, rather than a missal, and contains a number of rites for the Mass, for baptism, visiting the sick and anointing the dying. The last three folios contain a short treatise on the Mass in Old Irish, while on the final page are three prayers 'against injury to the eye, thorns, and disease of the urine'. It was compiled by five different scribes, and is mainly in Latin, with some Gaelic. The manuscript was annotated in the mid-eleventh century, when some pages were re-written, at the monastery of Lorrha in Tipperary.

Other writings influenced by the *Céli Dé* include the *Alphabet of Piety* (*Apgitir Chrábaid*) written at Lismore in the first half of the eighth century. This is based on John Cassian, and offers guidelines for a holy life, such as purity:

> In whom does the Holy Spirit dwell? In him who is pure, without sin. Then it is that a man is a vessel of the Holy Spirit, when the virtues come to replace vices. Then it is that desire for God increases in a man, when worldly desires wither.[5]

Another work is *Saltair na Rann*, a collection of 150 Irish poems on subjects from the Old Testament and the life of Christ. The *Céli Dé* also appear to have encouraged hermits to write poetry on themes including the natural world around them. The *Old Irish Penitential* was written in Tallaght in about 800; it was compiled 150 years after the Penitentials of Finnian, Cummíne and Columbanus. The three earlier examples are in Latin; this one is written in the vernacular.

Fighting the demons

The struggle to attain perfection which concerned the *Céli Dé* was not seen in purely human terms, for early monks believed they were part of a greater struggle against evil powers. St Paul had written: 'It is not against human enemies that we have to struggle, but against the Sovereignties and Powers who originate the darkness in this world, the spiritual army of evil in the heavens' (Eph. 6. 12). Jesus had told his followers to cast out devils (Mk. 16. 18), and said that difficult demons could be vanquished only by prayer and fasting (Mt. 17. 21), and Celtic monks took this task seriously: the weapons of prayer and fasting enabled them to fight against demons.

Night demons
In their understanding of demons, monks drew on Classical literature, Irish mythology and the Christian scriptures to create a fascinating amalgam

of beliefs. Every night, monks chanted psalm 91, entitled 'A song for evil encounters which should be recited before sleep': this was in order to protect them from demonic 'terrors of the night'. They prayed:

> He who dwells in the shelter of the Most High
> and abides in the shade of the Almighty
> says to the Lord, 'My refuge'.
> His truth will surround you with a shield.
> You will not fear the terrors of the night
> nor the arrow that flies by day,
> nor the plague that prowls in the darkness
> nor the noonday demon (Ps. 91, vv. 1, 5 ,6).[6]

The Old Testament love poems entitled 'The Song of Songs' were written in about the fifth century BC. They describe the sixty warriors who surround King Solomon's litter at night, with swords at the ready to defend him, not against human foes but against the same demons of the night:

> See ... the litter of Solomon.
> Around it are sixty champions
> All holding swords and most expert in war:
> every man's sword upon his thigh
> because of the terrors of the night (Song of Songs 3. 8).

This was also a familiar scene in early Irish literature.[7] The Old Testament story of Tobias and the Archangel Raphael in the Book of Tobit describes how couples were vulnerable to demons, especially on their wedding night (Tobit 7. 14-8. 20).

The *morrígan*

Church Fathers described a sexual demon, which they sometimes named Lilith, to be prayed against at night. In Jewish thought, Lilith seduced men and killed babies; she had long hair, and lived in lonely places. Lilith is referred to in the Book of Isaiah; when Jerome translated the Hebrew into Latin, he equated her with a monster named *Lamía*:

> And demons will meet ass-centaurs
> and the hairy creatures shall cry out, one to the other.
> There the Lamía has lain down and found rest for herself (Is. 34. 14, Vulgate).

In a ninth-century Irish manuscript of the Book of Isaiah, a gloss explains that *Lamía* is in fact a monster familiar to the Celtic world, which frequently appears in Irish poetry, a *morrígan*: '*Lamía* is a monster in the form of a woman, that is, a *morrígan*.'[8] Since Irish poetry was written by monks, they were familiar with this evolution of demonic monsters.

The role of the *morrígan* was to influence the outcome of war, often by flying overhead as a crow, to inspire either fear or courage in warriors fighting below. She also appeared to a particular warrior as a premonition of his imminent death; this suggests a link with the *banshee* of later Irish folklore.

Because the *morrígan* was a phantom of the night, she had to disappear at dawn. Blackbirds were observed to start singing before other birds, half an hour before sunrise, and so the blackbird's song was seen as a warning that the *morrígan* must soon disappear.[9] This is one reason why blackbirds feature in Irish monastic poetry: they proclaim that darkness must vanish before Christ, the Rising Sun.

The Eucharist

The most significant event of the monastic week was the gathering of the community to celebrate Eucharist each Sunday morning. In Patristic theology, and indeed that of Catholic Christians today, heaven and earth are united in this experience. In the Mass, God interacts with his people; they are redeemed at every Eucharist. The Mass is the point at which Calvary and the present moment converge. During the Eucharist, believers eat and drink with Christ at the Last Supper; simultaneously they stand at the foot of the cross, and meet Christ in the garden on Easter morning. When the priest says 'This is my body, which will be given up for you', he becomes Christ offering himself to the Father.

The short treatise in Old Irish at the end of the *Stowe Missal* invites monks to enter into this mystery. When the priest breaks the host, or wafer, in half and places it on the shallow metal dish, or paten, he is invited to reflect:

> The host on the paten [is] Christ's flesh on the tree of the cross. The fraction [of the host] on the paten is the breaking of his body with nails on the cross. The meeting wherewith the two halves [of the host] are joined after the fraction [is] a symbol of the entirety of Christ's body after the resurrection.

When the monks receive the host, they are invited to taste it before swallowing it, in order to savour this mystery: 'It is not meet to swallow the particle without tasting it, as it is improper not to seek to bring savours into God's mysteries.'

In later medieval thought, when Mary wrapped the child Jesus in swaddling clothes and laid him in a manger, this foreshadowed the dead Christ wrapped in a shroud and laid in a tomb. Christ hidden in the form of bread, placed on the altar linen at Mass recalled both scenes.[10] In the *Stowe Missal* tract, monks are invited to make similar connections:

The host, then, on the altar, … a symbol of Christ's body which has been set in the linen sheet of Mary's womb … The raising of the chalice … is a commemoration of Christ's birth and of his glory [seen] through signs and miracles.

Worthy reception of Communion

Because the Eucharist was considered to be so powerful, the *Céli Dé* allowed monks to receive it only occasionally, until they had lived in the monastery for a very long time. The first year, a novice at Tallaght was allowed to receive Communion only once, on Easter night; even then, he could only eat the bread and was not to drink the wine. After seven years, he was allowed to drink from the chalice, and after nine years, he could receive Communion every Sunday.

This is explained in *The Teaching of Máelrúain*:

The body of Christ, but not the chalice, was given to those who attended the midnight [Easter] Mass, and even this was not given until the end of the first year of conversion. At the end of this year, they went to midnight Mass at Easter and received the Body of Christ, but the chalice was not allowed them. In the third year they attended midnight Mass and received the Body of Christ alone at Easter and Christmas. In the fourth year they received the Body of Christ alone at Christmas, Easter, Low Sunday [at the end of Easter week] and Pentecost. In the fifth year the Body alone was granted them on the feasts above mentioned, and every forty days. In the sixth year they received the Body of Christ alone at the end of each month. In the seventh year this privilege was granted them on alternate Sundays. After nine years they were allowed to communicate every Sunday.[11]

Restricted access to the chalice may have been due to the fear of holiness being spread indiscriminately, before a person was ready for such an experience.[12] The eighth- or ninth-century Derrynaflan Chalice, which comes from a *Céli Dé* monastery in south Tipperary, is big enough to hold wine for a considerable congregation; this suggests that a large number of monks had lived there for more than ten years.

Baking the host

The host used for Mass was baked within the monastery. The treatise at the end of the *Stowe Missal* gives detailed instructions about how to divide the host, and what each particle symbolised. At the major feasts of Easter, Christmas and Pentecost, the host was large, because almost everyone was allowed to receive it. At Terryglass, it was divided into sixty-five particles, which were carefully arranged on the paten in the form of a cross:

Sixty-five … that is the number of particles that is in the host of Easter, Christmas and Whitsunday, for all is comprised in Christ … The arrangement of the confraction at Easter and at Christmas: thirteen particles in the stem of the cross, nine on its cross-piece, twenty particles in its circle-wheel; five particles in each angle. The middle particle is that to which the celebrant goes … What is from upwards of the shaft to the bishops, the cross piece on the left hand to the priests; that on the right to all the lesser clerics; that from the cross-piece down to the hermits and penitents …

Thus the celebrant was to consume the central particle, and the other pieces were carefully distributed to the bishops, priests, clerics in lesser orders, hermits and penitents, young clerics, 'innocent children', married folk and first communicants. The diagram below, showing how the host was possibly apportioned, is based on illustrations in the *Lindisfarne Gospels*, the *Book of Kells* and *the Book of Durrow*.

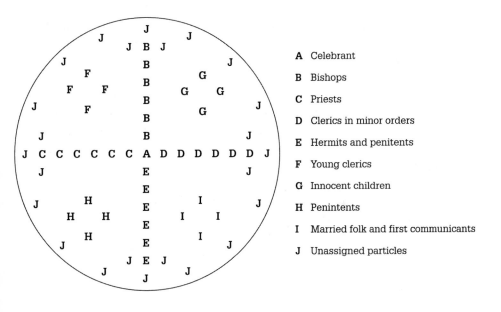

A Celebrant

B Bishops

C Priests

D Clerics in minor orders

E Hermits and penitents

F Young clerics

G Innocent children

H Penintents

I Married folk and first communicants

J Unassigned particles

The division of the host at Christmas and Easter, according to the Stowe Missal.

This complex symbolism was imposed on what was a simple, practical task: how to divide a loaf into enough pieces for everyone. This had to be done neatly, and when monks viewed the resulting arrangement, they devised an allegory about what it 'meant'.

The imposition of an added layer of symbolic meaning onto the host at Mass was not unique to Celtic monks. The Coptic monks of Egypt still prepare the Holy Bread for Easter in a similar way: the loaf must be circular, to symbolise God, who has no beginning or end. In the middle of the loaf, a circle is inscribed, together with the words 'Holy God, holy Mighty, holy Immortal'. Around the words are five holes, to represent the five wounds of Jesus on the cross, in his hands, feet and side. Inside the circle, twelve small crosses represent the apostles gathered at the Last Supper. Today, the Coptic Easter liturgy lasts almost five hours.

Dietary laws

Ritual purity was important to the *Céli Dé*. Jesus had said 'Be perfect as my heavenly Father is perfect' (Mt. 5. 48), and he appeared to encourage strict adherence to laws:

> Do not imagine that I have come to abolish the Law or the Prophets. I have come not to abolish but to complete them. I tell you solemnly, till heaven and earth disappear, not one dot, not one little stroke, shall disappear from the Law until its purpose is achieved. (Mt. 5. 17-18).

Celtic monks were familiar with the many dietary laws enumerated in the Old Testament Book of Leviticus and elsewhere. For the *Céli Dé*, keeping to regulations with regard to food became symbolic of the perfect monk, and organising the monastic kitchen became almost obsessional.

One third of the ninety chapters in the collection entitled *The Monastery of Tallaght* concern food and drink. Monks were to feed themselves in a way that enabled them to pray well, and rules were to be adjusted to individual needs, with surprising freedom: 'Every man should regulate his pittance for himself. It should be limited to men's natures, for the course of nature differs in each man'. In some communities, meat was forbidden, except for a single morsel on Easter day: this was in order to keep the body accustomed to meat, which might have to be eaten if the crops failed, and in order to counteract pride, so that no monk could boast that he was vegetarian.

Physical enjoyment of food was regarded as sinful. Máelrúain forbade beer, and challenged Dublittir's opinion that it should sometimes be allowed; however, Dublittir replied that his monks would also enter paradise. The main foods were bread and porridge, to which the abbot sometimes added extra butter for the monks' health. Food was rarely stored; any left over was given to the poor. On Sundays, no food could be gathered; fasting was forbidden on Sunday, the day of Christ's resurrection.

There were restrictions on drinking when thirsty, but a jug of water was available when fasting on bread and water. Water and whey were allowed in small quantities, but milk was rarely permitted. The comparative merits of strict fasting versus a small but regular allowance of food are discussed in *The Monastery of Tallaght*. Types and grades of gruel are enumerated; eating too soon is forbidden. The allowance of food for elderly monks is described, and the degree of abstinence they should undertake. In early times, when health care was less skilled, appropriate care of the infirm must have posed particular problems.

Céli Dé beyond Ireland

The *Céli Dé* spread to Wales and Scotland, where they survived throughout medieval times; here, they were often referred to as Culdees. There is archaeological evidence of a *Céli Dé* community in south Wales at Burry Holms, an island off the western tip of the Gower peninsula, and penitential poems in *The Black Book of Carmarthen* resemble Irish *Céli Dé* poetry. Llanbadarn Fawr, a monastery south of Aberystwyth on the west coast of Wales, had close links with Ireland, and may have become a reformed Culdee community: unlike other monasteries in south-west Wales, Llanbadarn Fawr became a centre of learning.[13]

St David's
In Pembrokeshire in south-west Wales, St David's may also have been a monastery of the *Céli Dé*. Most of our knowledge of its community comes from Rhygyfarch's *Life of David*, written in Latin around 1095 and preserved in a copy of about 1200. While this is a late text, it preserves earlier information, since Rhygyfarch's father, Sulien, was Bishop of St David's for ten years, and was therefore acquainted with traditions about its founder.

Nine paragraphs in the *Life*, based on an early source, describe how David and his followers lived: the monks grew their own food, working hard with mattocks, hoes and axes. They were to plough the fields themselves, instead of using oxen. This may refer to the saying of Jesus in the Gospels: 'Once the hand is laid on the plough, no one who looks back is fit for the kingdom of God' (Lk. 9. 62); it was perhaps an attempt to carry this out in reality.

The monks were to spend the remainder of each day reading, writing and praying. In the evening, the chapel bell summoned them to sing vespers, chanting the psalms 'with heart and voice in complete harmony'. They then prayed silently until nightfall, when at last they were allowed to eat together, but only 'bread and herbs seasoned with salt', taken in moderation, and washed down with ale.[14]

Latin cross, St David's, Pembrokeshire.

The community then returned to chapel for silent prayer, and remained 'in vigils, prayers and genuflections for about three hours'. After a short night's sleep, they woke at cockcrow to sing matins and to 'spend the rest of the night until morning without sleep'. They wore simple clothes, mostly of animal skins. They were to own nothing, giving away all their possessions before being allowed to join the community, and so entered the monastery 'naked, as if escaping from a shipwreck'.[15]

There is an interesting reference to David in a *Life of Paul Aurélian* written by a monk named Gourmonoc at Landévennec in Brittany in 884. Gourmonoc tells us that David was nicknamed *Aquaticus* ('water-drinker') because he lived on bread, vegetables and water alone. The austerity of David and his monks over several centuries suggests that St David's became a centre of the *Céli Dé*.

Rhygyfarch's father Sulien studied in Ireland, where he could have encountered these reforming monks, before he became bishop of St David's in 1073. If St David's were a *Céli Dé* community, this might explain its continued ascetic lifestyle.[16] David himself died 200 years before Máelrúain of Tallaght but, as we have seen, early Irish monasteries were influenced by those of south Wales, so it may be that the rigorous lifestyle at St David's affected the development of the *Céli Dé* in Ireland. Little survives from early times at St David's; however, the Latin cross seen above is one of a number of seventh- to ninth-century grave markers from the Celtic monastery.

The *Céli Dé* in north Wales

Writing in the twelfth century, Gerald of Wales tells us of three reformed *Céli Dé* monasteries in north Wales. One was at Penmon at the north-eastern tip of Anglesey, 3 miles north-north-east of Beaumaris; its first abbot was Seiriol, nephew of Einion, Prince of Lleyn. Here can be found the most complete monk's hermitage to survive in Wales: the circular stone wall of a monk's hut rests snugly against a sheltering cliff (*colour plate 21*). Beside it are remains of a well chapel and its antechamber, with stone seats where a few people could gather; the brickwork over the well dates from the eighteenth century. The present church was built by Celtic monks in the twelfth century to replace one burnt by the Danes in 971. Two fine tenth-century crosses are preserved inside the church.

There was a second Culdee monastery at Beddgelert, at the foot of Mount Snowdon. Writing in his *Speculum Ecclesiae* in about 1220, Gerald of Wales observes:

> In Gwynedd ... there was a religious house of clerics at the foot of the mountain of Eryri, commonly called the Mountain of Snows [Snowdon] ... Here there were clerics devoted to the service of God and living in a holy manner and in common, after the example of the Apostles. They were not bound to any order of monks or canons but were celibates or Culdees, who served God and were given to abstinence, continence and renowned for their charity and hospitality.[17]

The group eventually accepted the Augustinian Rule; nothing survives today from the early monastery.

The third *Céli Dé* monastery in north Wales was on Bardsey Island (*colour plate 22*). The Welsh name for Bardsey is *Ynys Enlli* ('Island in the Current'). It lies only 2 miles offshore, but because of the strong currents in the Sound, the sea journey can be as much as 6 miles. Writing in 1188, Gerald of Wales

Site of early monastery, Bardsey Island, Gwynned.

described the '*coelibes* [celibates] of Ynys Enlli who were also called *colidei* [*Céli Dé*]'.[18] It is not known whether a monastery was continuously occupied on Bardsey in Celtic times; it may have been used only as a Lenten retreat by monks living on the mainland at Aberdaron, or at nearby Capel Anelog, where two gravestones were found dating from the late fifth or early sixth century. The tombstones refer to two priests and 'many brothers'.

On Bardsey Island, graves which may be those of early monks are clustered around the ruined tower of a thirteenth-century Augustinian monastery. There are also circular foundations of monks' huts, of indeterminate date. The earliest reference to the monastery is a record of the death of a monk in 1011. The steward of the thirteenth-century community was given the title *Oeconomus*, an early Greek word originating with the desert monks of the Near East. This archaic title may have been used in earlier times by Celtic monks on Bardsey.[19]

Bardsey is a Norse name meaning 'Bardr's Island': in the tenth century it perhaps became the base of a Viking pirate chief. If so, the monks would have fled, or been killed or kidnapped. They appear to have returned, however, for the lower half of a cross dating from the late tenth or early eleventh century depicts a monk wearing a pleated robe which almost reaches his ankles.[20] In medieval times, Bardsey was called the 'Isle of the Saints' after the monks who were buried here; it became a famous centre for pilgrimage. Today, hermits once more live and pray on the island.

Culdees in Scotland

From the twelfth century until the fourteenth, Scottish records refer to the presence of Culdees (or *keledei*) at St Andrews, Dunkeld and in other locations,[21] chiefly in Angus and Fife. Near the east coast of Angus, 25 miles north-east of Dundee, Brechin Cathedral became a Culdee church in the tenth century, under King Kenneth II. A round tower was constructed in the Irish style at this time.

There was another Culdee foundation on the picturesque Isle of Loch Leven, 7 miles west of Glenrothes in Fife: The *Life of St Serf* relates that a certain King Brude (we are unsure which) 'gave the Isle of Loch Leven to God and St Serf and to the Culdee hermits who lived there'. This is said to have taken place in the first half of the eighth century. We are told that Serf remained here for seven years with the Culdee monks; the community continued until the twelfth century. Its priests were well accepted, and some of them held office at St Peter's in York until 936. Canons at St Peter's were referred to as Culdees until the reign of King Henry II in the mid-twelfth century.[22]

St Andrews

The Celtic name for St Andrews, on the Fife coast, was Kilrimont, or 'church of the king's mound; this suggests the presence of a royal fort. There are traditions of a monk named Rule who lived in a cave by the shore, now known as Lady Buchan's Cave. The monastery is first recorded in 747, when Irish annals note the death of its abbot. Fifteen years earlier, in 732, Bishop Acca of Hexham was driven from his diocese and came to live at Kilrimont. He brought with him relics of St Andrew which his predecessor, Wilfrid, had obtained from Rome. The precious relics of the apostle enhanced the prestige of Kilrimont, which was later renamed St Andrews.[23]

In 943, King Constantine II retired from office and became abbot of Kilrimont's monastic community; the church of St Rule was built to serve its monks. King Alexander I, who reigned from 1107 to 1124, attempted to convert the Culdee monks of Kilrimont to Roman ways. He tried to appoint a bishop who would help him to reform the community, but the first two bishops he chose were unwilling to do so. The King achieved a measure of success with his third candidate, Robert, Prior of the Augustinian abbey of Scone. Bishop Robert determined to establish a group of Augustinian canons at Kilrimont, who would transform it into a model Roman cathedral chapter.

The Culdee monks opposed their new bishop so fiercely, however, that Robert was unable to carry out his plans until 1144, over twenty years later. The Celtic clergy, consisting of about thirteen monks and some priests, all of them married, were invited to join the new community, but they declined. They were given a permanent home in the church of St Mary on the Rock, whose foundations can be seen outside the cathedral walls, close to the shore. The building was on the edge of the promontory, overlooking the harbour (*colour plate 23*). Many of the carved cross slabs now in the visitor centre were found here. In 1248 the community at St Mary of the Rock was recognised as an independent college of diocesan priests.[24]

Céli Dé: a group apart

This was not an unusual arrangement: the Culdees had a strong sense of identity, and were used to living alongside, yet separate from, other monks. While they established some monasteries of their own, like that of Tallaght, at other foundations such as Roscrea, Tipperary, in central Ireland, they created a separate adjoining community. At Armagh in the north, however, the *Céli Dé* formed a group who lived within the monastic enclosure and followed a stricter lifestyle than the monks around them.[25] This may have led to uncomfortable comparisons and conflicts, but the *Céli Dé* were idealists, who believed uncompromisingly in their ideals

Because the *Céli Dé* lacked firm structures, the movement began to lose impetus from the mid-ninth century onwards. However it left behind an unmistakable legacy, a commitment to personal holiness, study and prayer. It also developed the use of the Irish language, alongside Latin. The term *Céli Dé* in its Gaelic and Latin forms remained in use as late as the seventeenth century in Ireland, although by then the term had altered considerably in meaning.[26]

Carving of a Céli Dé *monk, Killadeas, Fermanagh.*

The spirit of the *Céli Dé*

The *Céli De* community on Devenish Island in Lough Erne was described in Chapter 10, together with its daughter house on the mainland at Killadeas whose name, as we saw, is a transliteration of *Céli Dé*. The so-called Bishop's Stone in Killadeas graveyard may be the only surviving representation of the superior of a known *Céli Dé* community. He leans on his staff and rings a bell to summon his monks to prayer. His grave deportment and his focussed steps well convey the attitudes cultivated by the *Céli Dé*; this elderly monk has spent a lifetime learning holiness.

His pastoral staff tells us, perhaps, that he has acquired the wisdom to shepherd others, while his large bell would ring out across the monastic enclosure and beyond. St David named his bell *bangu*, or 'dear loud one'; he evidently considered it a friend. The monk carved on the stone at Killadeas looks serious because he is focused on the inner life, rather than the outer life. Yet, as we saw in Chapter 1, Antony of Egypt emerged 'radiant, ... inspired by God' from his years of spiritual struggle in the desert, and Celtic monks and nuns sought the same radiance.

Abbess Samthann

The carving at Killadeas does not, however, convey human warmth. For a gentler and more friendly approach to monastic life, we must turn to Samthann, who appears to have been abbess of a Céli Dé monastery of women, 40 miles south of Killadeas. Samthann (d. 793) is one of only four Irish women saints whose Latin *vitae* survive, the others being three sixth-century saints, Brigit, Íte and Monenna. Samthann's *Life* survives in three manuscripts, the most complete being an early fourteenth-century text in the Bodleian Library.[27]

Although this is a late source, it appears to have been copied from an early ninth-century original, written within a few decades of Samthann's death, at her monastery of Clonbroney in Meath, just east of present-day Longford. The use of individual names mentioned in the *Life*, together with the monastery's association with the royal family of Tethba, in Cairpre Gabra, both suggest an early date for the text.

Genealogies indicate that Samthann came from Ulster. After avoiding marriage to a nobleman, Samthann joined a women's monastery at Urney in Tyrone, where she became its steward. After her death we hear of Urney as a monastery of monks, rather than nuns. According to her *Life*, Fuinnech, abbess of Clonbroney, saw a vision depicting Samthann's holiness, after which she sent for her; Samthann then replaced her as abbess.[28] Clonbroney subsequently faded from history; it is no longer mentioned in records after the death of its abbess Caillechdomhnaill in 1163.

One reason why Clonbroney did not become a famous monastery may have been its poverty. While Brigit's monastery at Kildare became very wealthy, Samthann would not accept estates for her community, nor a large herd of cows. The author of her *Life* comments: 'She refused to hold fields; nor did she ever have more than six cows at a time. Thus all goods, and especially her own household items, were solicited through charity.'[29] It also appears that the monastery owned no sheep, for the *Life* describes some monks from Iona sailing to Ireland with a boatload of wool for her community; this would enable them to weave their habits.[30]

Samthann and the *Céli Dé*

The abbess was highly regarded by *Céli Dé* monks. She asked for either Máelrúain or Férdacrích, abbot of Devenish (we are unsure which), both leaders of the movement, to be her soul-friend, which the monk considered to be an honour. There is a hymn in honour of Samthann in the margin of the *Martyrology of Tallaght*, and her name is included in both a litany in the *Stowe Missal*, and in the main body of the text. She features in the text of *The Monastery of Tallaght*. Since women were often regarded with suspicion by *Céli Dé* monks, Samthann must have been outstanding for her holiness and learning.

Her teaching echoes *Céli Dé* themes: she held study in high regard, and did not favour *peregrinatio*, or pilgrimage. Her *Life* records a visit by a well-known monk, Daircellach 'the wise', who died in 760, according to the *Annals of Ulster*. The author of Samthann's *Life* relates:

Daircellach the teacher came to the virgin, and told her, 'I propose to defer study and cease from prayer.' She said to him 'What, then, can steady your mind lest it stray, if you shall have neglected spiritual cultivation?' The sage responded, 'I wish to go on pilgrimage.' She retorted, 'If God is not to be found on this side of the sea, certainly we may go abroad. For since God is near all who summon him, no need of voyaging besets us. One can reach heaven from any place on earth.'[31]

Samthann's *Life* relates how another monk asked what postures were appropriate for prayer, to which she replied: 'In every position, standing, sitting or lying down'. This is perhaps intended to summarise the *Shema*, which Jews repeat every night and morning, from the Book of Deuteronomy: 'Let these words ... be written on your heart. You shall repeat them ... whether at rest in your house or walking abroad, at your lying down or at your rising' (Deut. 6. 7). Both Samthann and the unknown monk are likely to have been familiar with this text.

Her human warmth
Perhaps Samthann's years as monastic steward taught her the value of generosity. Unlike the serious cleric depicted at Killadeas, she enjoyed making others smile. Her *Life* recounts that, when she became abbess of Clonbroney, she found that her workmen were hungry:

> After she had taken charge, first she wanted to construct an oratory of trimmed timber, and so she sent out carpenters and other workmen to bring in timber from forests nearby. One of the carpenters, observing the paucity of provisions and the number of workers, thought to himself, 'Oh, if only we could have forty wheaten loaves with butter and cheese and milk; for such a quantity of bread would suffice us!' ... Through the merits of holy Samthann, all he had thought, he saw placed before him. The intimate of Christ, giggling, said, 'The thought of your heart is fulfilled, is it not?' ... Then all gave thanks to God and his servant, and ate their fill.[32]

The story recalls how Jesus fed the 5000 in the desert with five barley loaves and a few fish (Jn. 6. 5-14); it also echoes the Old Testament account of the prophet Elisha feeding the brotherhood with twenty barley loaves and fresh grain in the ear (2 Kg. 4. 42-4).

Other stories of her generosity with food, even when it was scarce, form a welcome balance to the meagre allowance prescribed at *Céli Dé* men's monasteries. In her early days as the steward at Urney, through her blessing, 'one vat of butter was sufficient for the sisters and their guests for a whole year'. In another anecdote, 'She was said to have once fed fifty guests with the milk of a single cow, whom she milked'. And again, 'At another time, she fed the abbot of Devenish and 140 others with food and drink for a week, with a single measure of flour divided into two parts'.[33] A visit from the abbot of a *Céli Dé* monastery 40 miles to the north indicates the degree of respect which was given to Samthann.

Other stories describe her political interventions, which were motivated by compassion. A man whom a king had defeated and imprisoned was set free by her prayers. Hostages were released at her request; in one instance, she sent her prioress to bring about the liberation of a hostage.[34]

Perhaps because she was a woman, the author of Samthann's *Life* felt able to offer a warmer, more humane viewpoint of life in a *Céli Dé* community than we find in other texts. Yet the aim of both monks and nuns was to live in union with God, at peace with themselves, with others and with the entire natural world. Their desire was to become divinised, and so become fully human since, in the words of the second-century theologian, Irenaeus, 'the glory of God is a person, fully alive'.[35] Their concern with the daily details of how to live a holy life may appear a little eccentric to us, 1200 years later, but their ultimate aim was clear and true.

NOTES

1. Saints in the desert

1. Unless stated otherwise, scripture quotations are from *The Jerusalem Bible*, ed. A. Jones (London, Darton, Longman and Todd, 1968).
2. *Vita Antoniae*, 7, J.P. Migne, *Patrologia Graeca* (Paris, 1857–66), vol. 26, cols. 839–975, transl. M. Groves and R. Walls in *Life of Saint Antony* (Vanve, France, Aide Inter-Monastères, 1994), p. 22.
3. Moses, no. 6, in *The Sayings of the Desert Fathers: the Alphabetical Collection*, ed. and transl. B. Ward (London, Mowbray, 1981), p. 139.
4. B. Ward, *The Wisdom of the Desert Fathers:* Apothegmata Patrum *from the Anonymous Series* (Oxford, SLG Press, 1981), no. 72, p. 24.
5. *Vita Antoniae*, 7, transl. M. Groves and R. Walls in *Life of Saint Antony*, p. 22.
6. Isaiah, 2, in *The Sayings of the Desert Fathers: the Alphabetical Collection*, B. Ward, p. 69.
7. *Vitae Patrum* V and VI, bk. 10, no. 7, in T. Merton, transl., *The Wisdom of the Desert* (Kentucky, Abbey of Gethsemani, 1960). See H. Waddell, ed. and transl., *The Desert Fathers* (London, Fontana, 1962), p. 110, for a slightly different translation.
8. Poeman, no. 189, in *The Sayings of the Desert Fathers: the Alphabetical Collection*, B. Ward, p. 193.
9. *Vitae Patrum* V and VI, bk. 8, no. 17, in H. Waddell, *The Desert Fathers*, p. 108.
10. Anthony the Great, no. 27, *The Sayings of the Desert Fathers: the Alphabetical Collection*, B. Ward, p. 7.
11. M. Driot, *Fathers of the Desert* (Slough, St Paul Publications, 1992), p. 17.
12. John the Dwarf, no. 31, in *The Alphabetical Collection*, in M. Driot, *Fathers of the Desert*, p. 66.
13. B. Ward, *The Wisdom of the Desert Fathers*, no. 18, p. 5.
14. Poeman, no. 92, in *The Sayings of the Desert Fathers: the Alphabetical Collection*, B. Ward, p. 179.
15. M. Driot, *Fathers of the Desert*, p. 88.
16. 'The Additions of Rufinus to the *Historia Monachorum*', in *The Lives of the Desert Fathers*, transl. N. Russell (London, Mowbray, 1981), p. 153.

17. *Vitae Patrum* V and VI, bk. 10, no. 15, in H. Waddell, *The Desert Fathers*, p. 112.
18. *Vitae Patrum* V and VI, bk. 7, no. 5, in H. Waddell, *The Desert Fathers*, p. 101.
19. B. Ward, *The Wisdom of the Desert Fathers*, no. 22, p. 6.
20. Cassian, *Conferences* no. 7. 26 in M. Driot, *Fathers of the Desert*, p. 54.
21. *Vita Antoniae*, 28, transl. M. Groves and R. Walls in *Life of Saint Antony*, p. 53.
22. M. Driot, *Fathers of the Desert*, p. 129.
23. Pambo, no. 10, in *The Sayings of the Desert Fathers: the Alphabetical Collection*, B. Ward, p. 197.
24. Joseph of Panephysis, no. 7, in *The Sayings of the Desert Fathers: the Alphabetical Collection*, B. Ward, p. 103.
25. B. Ward, *The Wisdom of the Desert Fathers*, no. 151, p. 42.
26. Rufinus, *Historium Monachorum in Aegypto*; Latin version in J. P. Migne (ed.), *Patrologia Latina* (Paris, 1844 onwards), vol. 21, cols. 387–462.
27. In J. Wilkinson, *Egeria's Travels* (London, SPCK, 1973), pp. 175–6.
28. J. Wilkinson, *Egeria's Travels*, pp. 94–6.
29. *The New Revised Standard Version of the Bible* (Nashville, Tenessee, Thomas Nelson, 1989).
30. *Vita Antoniae*, 14, transl. M. Groves and R. Walls in *Life of Saint Antony*, p. 32.
31. E.G. Bowen, *Saints, Seaways and Settlements in the Celtic Lands* (Cardiff, Cardiff University Press, 1969), pp. 133–5.

2. Patrick and his followers

1. C. Thomas, *And Shall These Mute Stones Speak?* (Cardiff, Cardiff University Press, 1994), pp. 28–30.
2. R.A.S. Macalister, *Corpus Inscriptionum Insularum Celticarum*, vol. 1 (Dublin, The Stationery Office, 1945), pp. 258–60.
3. Ps. 95. 6; Ps. 110. 3; Ps. 148. 14; Heb. 4. 14. See O. Davies, *Celtic Spirituality*, in *Classics of Western Spirituality* Series (New Jersey, Paulist Press, 1999), pp. 28–9.
4. K. Jankulak, 'Patrick and the Patrick Tradition', lecture at Lampeter University, June 2004.
5. Patrick, *Confessio*, 16, in T. O'Loughlin, *Saint Patrick: the Man and his Works* (London, SPCK, 1999), pp. 60–61.
6. Patrick, *Confessio*, 46, in T. O'Loughlin, p. 80.
7. Patrick, *Confessio*, 6, in T. O'Loughlin, p. 69.
8. K. Jankulak, 'Patrick and the Patrick Tradition'.
9. Patrick, *Confessio*, 18, 19, in T. O'Loughlin, pp. 62–3.
10. Patrick, *Confessio*, 23, in T. O'Loughlin, p. 66.
11. Patrick, *Confessio*, 32, in T. O'Loughlin, p. 71.
12. Patrick, *Confessio*, 51, 14, in T. O'Loughlin, pp. 83, 60.
13. Patrick, *Confessio*, 38, in T. O'Loughlin, p. 75.
14. Patrick, *Confessio*, 41, 42, in T. O'Loughlin, pp. 77–8.
15. Patrick, *Confessio*, 40, in T. O'Loughlin, p. 76.
16. Patrick, *Confessio*, 43, in T. O'Loughlin, p. 78.
17. Patrick, *Confessio*, 55, in T. O'Loughlin, p. 85.
18. Patrick, *Confessio*, 61, in T. O'Loughlin, p. 89.
19. T. O'Loughlin, *Journeys to the Edges: The Celtic Tradition* (London, Darton, Longman and Todd, 2000), pp. 88–90.
20. E.G. Bowen, *Saints, Seaways and Settlements in the Celtic Lands* (Cardiff, Cardiff University Press, 1969), pp. 126–7.

21. Adomnán, *Vita Columbae*, bk. 2, ch. 5, in J. Marsden, *The Illustrated Columcille* (London, Macmillan, 1991), pp. 106–7.
22. Adomnán, *Vita Columbae*, second Preface.
23. M. Herity, *Gleanncholmcille* (Dublin, Michael Herity, 1998), pp. 44, 47.
24. H.G. Leask and H. A. Wheeler, *St Patrick's Rock, Cashel* (Dublin, Stationery Office, n. d.), pp. 2–3.
25. H.G. Leask and H. A. Wheeler, *St Patrick's Rock, Cashel*, pp. 24–5.
26. Information at the site, 2011.
27. Information at the site, 2011.

3. Some island monasteries

1. T. O'Loughlin, 'Authority and Asceticism in early Irish Monasticism', lecture at Lampeter University, June 2003.
2. T. O'Loughlin, 'Authority and Asceticism in early Irish Monasticism'.
3. Information at the site, 2011.
4. Information at the site, 2011.
5. Information at the site, 2011.
6. G. Madden, *Holy Island; Inis Cealtra* (Mountshannon, Clare, Holy Island Tours, 2008), p. 23.
7. G. Madden, *Holy Island, Jewel of the Lough: a history* (Tuamgraney, Clare, East Clare Heritage, 2004), p. 6.
8. G. Madden, *Holy Island; Inis Cealtra*, pp. i, 2–3, 38.
9. Information at the site, 2011.
10. G. Madden, *Holy Island; Inis Cealtra*, pp. 7–8.
11. D. Lavelle, *The Skellig Story: an ancient monastic outpost* (Dublin, O'Brien Press, 2004), p. 42.
12. D. Lavelle, *The Skellig Story*, p. 10.
13. J. Wooding, 'Monastic Communities in the Celtic West', lecture at Lampeter University, June 2008.
14. J. Wooding, 'Searching for the "desert" on land and sea', lecture at Lampeter University, June 2003.
15. G. Moorhouse, *Sun Dancing: a Medieval Vision* (London, Weidenfield & Nicholson, 1997).

4. Brigit and other nuns

1. M. Low, 'Canaire of Inis Cathaig', in G. Markus (ed.), *The Radical Tradition* (London, Doubleday, 1993), p. 27.
2. St Patrick, *Confessio*, 41, 42 in T. O'Loughlin, *Saint Patrick: the Man and his Works* (London, SPCK, 1999), pp. 77–8.
3. G. Winkler 'The Origins and idiosyncrasies of the earliest form of ascetiscism' in W. Studlarek, (ed.) *The Continuing Quest for God* (Collegeville, Minnesota, Liturgical Press, 1982).
4. A.C. Wire, *The Corinthian Women Prophets: a Reconstruction through Paul's Rhetoric* (Minneapolis, Fortress Press, 2003), pp. 181–7.
5. T. O'Loughlin, 'How Christians perceived Conversion', lecture at Lampeter University, June 2006.
6. Muirchú, *Dedication* to *The Life of Patrick*, quoted in O. Davies, *Celtic Spirituality* in *Classics of Western Spirituality* Series (New Jersey, Paulist Press, 1999), p. 91.

7. K. Jankulak, 'Brigid – Saint and Goddess', lecture at Lampeter University, June 2006.

8. K. Jankulak, 'Brigid – Saint and Goddess'.

9. O. Davies, *Celtic Spirituality* in *Classics of Western Spirituality* Series, p. 121.

10. W. Stokes (ed.) *Three Irish Glossaries: Cormac's Glossary, O'Davoren's Glossary and a Glossary to the Calendar of Oengus the Culdee* (London, Williams and Norgate, 1862), pp. 1–44.

11. A. Carmichael, *Carmina Gadelica* (Edinburgh, Floris, 1992), pp. 580–2.

12. E. Rees, *Christian Symbols, Ancient Roots* (London, Jessica Kingsley, 1992), pp. 28–31.

13. W.J. Watson, *The History of the Celtic Place-names of Scotland* (Edinburgh, Birlinn, 1993), p. 275.

14. K. Jankulak, 'St Íte', lecture at Lampeter University, June 2006.

15. K. Jankulak, 'St Íte'.

16. W. Stokes, (ed.), *Félire Óengusso Céli Dé: The Martyrology of Óengus the Culdee* (London, Henry Bradshaw Society, vol. 29, 1905; reprint, Dublin Institute for Advanced Studies, 1984).

17. E.G. Quin, 'The Early Irish Poem Ísucán', *Cambridge Medieval Celtic Studies*, vol. 1, 1981, pp. 39–52.

18. E.G. Quin, 'The Early Irish Poem Ísucán'.

19. K. Jankulak, 'St Íte'.

20. B. Duffy, *Archaeology in County Sligo* (Sligo, Duchás – the Heritage Service, 1998), p. 26.

21. B. Duffy, *Archaeology in County Sligo*, p. 26.

5. Early saints of Munster

1. D. Ó Riain-Raedel, 'The Question of the "Pre-Patrician Saints of Munster"', *Early Medieval Munster. Archaeology, History and Society*, ed. M.A. Monk and J. Sheehan (Cork, Cork University Press, 1998), pp. 20–21.

2. D. Ó Riain-Raedel, 'The Question of the "Pre-Patrician Saints of Munster"', pp. 20–21.

3. E. Johnstone 'Munster, saints of (active *c.* 450 – *c.* 700)' in *Oxford Dictionary of National Biography* (Oxford, Oxford University Press, 2004).

4. C. Plummer, (ed.), *Latin Life of Déclán*, *Vitae Sanctorum Hiberniae*, vol. 2 (Oxford, Oxford University Press, 1910); R. Sharpe, *Medieval Irish Saints' Lives: an Introduction to* Vitae Sanctorum Hiberniae (Oxford, Oxford University Press, 1991), p. 243 onwards.

5. R. Sharpe, *Medieval Irish Saints' Lives,* p. 243.

6. S. Lincoln, *Declan of Ardmore* (Cork, Aisling, 1995), p. 43.

7. R. Sharpe, *Medieval Irish Saints' Lives,* p. 243.

8. Information at the site, 2011.

9. *The Irish Life of Ciarán of Saighir*, ed. and transl. S.H. O'Grady, in *Silva Gadelica* (London and Edinburgh, Williams & Norgate, 1892).

10. K. Jankulak, 'Alba Longa in the Celtic regions? Swine, saints and Celtic hagiography' in *Celtic Hagiography and Saints' Cults*, ed. J. Cartwright (Cardiff, University of Wales Press, 2003), p. 271.

11. K. Jankulak, 'Alba Longa in the Celtic regions?', pp. 272–81.

12. O. Davies, (ed.), *Celtic Spirituality*, in *Classics of Western Spirituality* Series (New Jersey, Paulist Press, 1999), p. 100. Davies indicates the many scriptural allusions in this dialogue.

13. Information at the site, 2011.

14. Information at the site, 2011.

6. Victims of plague

1. T. O'Loughlin, 'The Celtic Perception of Time', lecture at Lampeter University, June 2004.
2. G.K. Kohn, *Encyclopedia of Plague and Pestilence*, 3rd edition (New York, Facts on File Books, 2010), p. 449.
3. B. Cunningham, (ed.), *The Annals of the Four Masters* (Dublin, Four Courts Press, 2010).
4. Bede, *Ecclesiastical History of the English People*, bk. 3, ch. 23.
5. Information at the site, 2011.
6. J.T. McNeill and H.M. Gamer, (eds.), *Medieval Handbooks of Penance* (New York, Columbia University Press, 1990), pp. 86–97.
7. Gildas, *Letter to Finnian*, in M. Winterbottom, *Gildas* (Chichester, Phillimore, 1980).
8. L. Bieler, *Sancti Columbani Opera, Scriptores Latini Hiberniae*, vol. 2 (Dublin, 1957); G.S.M. Walker (ed. and transl.), *Columbanus's Letters* (Dublin, 1979).
9. Adomnán, *Vita Columbae*, bk. 3, ch. 3, in J. Marsden, *The Illustrated Columcille* (London, Macmillan, 1991), p. 154.
10. J. Wooding, 'St Finnian, Gildas and the Celtic Church', lecture at Lampeter University, June 2004.
11. J. Wooding, 'St Finnian, Gildas and the Celtic Church'.
12. M. Richter, *New Gill History of Ireland*, vol. 1. *Medieval Ireland: the Enduring Tradition* (Dublin, Gill and Macmillan, revised ed., 2005), pp. 50–52.
13. C. Manning, *Clonmacnoise* (Dublin, Dúchas, 1998), p. 52.
14. C. Manning, *Early Irish Monasteries* (Dublin, Town House & Country House, 1995), p. 24.
15. Adomnán, *Vita Columbae*, bk. 1, ch. 3, in J. Marsden, *The Illustrated Columcille*, p. 60.
16. C. Manning, *Clonmacnoise*, p. 7.
17. C. Manning, *Clonmacnoise*, p. 36.
18. Information at the site, 2011.
19. Information at the site, 2011.
20. Information at the site, 2011.
21. Information at the site, 2011.
22. J.H. Bernard and R. Atkinson, *The Irish 'Liber Hymnorum'* (London, Henry Bradshaw Society, 1898), vol. 13.

7. Brendan the Navigator

1. C. Plummer (ed.), *Latin Lives of the Irish Saints, Vitae Sanctorum Hiberniae* (Oxford, Oxford University Press, 1910), vol. 1, p. 143.
2. W.J. Watson, *The History of the Celtic Place-names of Scotland* (Edinburgh, Birlinn, 1993), pp. 81–2.
3. Adomnán, *Vita Columbae*, bk. 3, ch. 16, in J. Marsden, *The Illustrated Columcille* (London, Macmillan, 1991), p. 165.
4. L. Bieler, *The Irish Penitentials* (Dublin, Dublin Institute for Advanced Studies, 1975), p. 113 onwards.
5. Information at the site, 2011.
6. Information at the site, 2011.
7. J. Wooding, 'Desert in the Ocean: vernacular voyage tales', lecture at Lampeter University, June 2007.

8. E. Rees, *Christian symbols, ancient roots* (London, Jessica Kingsley, 1992), pp. 40–1.
9. T. O'Loughlin, *Journeys on the Edges: The Celtic Tradition* (London, Darton, Longman and Todd, 2000), pp. 91–8.
10. J. Wooding, 'Geography and Celtic Theology', lecture at Lampeter University, June 2005.
11. J. Wooding, 'Monastic Community in the Celtic West: Desert in the Ocean', lecture at Lampeter University, June 2008.
12. J. Wooding, 'Irish and English Monks and Vikings: New reflections on the conversion of Scandinavia', lecture at Lampeter University, June 2005.
13. T. O'Loughlin, *Saint Patrick: The Man and his Works* (London, SPCK, 1999), pp. 42–7.
14. P. Harbison, *Ancient Irish Monuments* (Dublin, Gill & Macmillan, 1997), pp. 33–5.
15. Information at the site, 2011.
16. T. O'Loughlin, *Journeys to the Edges*, p. 6.

8. The Columban family

1. J. Dunbar and I. Fisher, *Iona: a Guide to the Monuments* (Edinburgh, Her Majesty's Stationery Office, 1995), p. 15.
2. Dunbar and Fisher, *Iona*, p. 13.
3. Dunbar and Fisher, *Iona*, p. 15.
4. Dunbar and Fisher, *Iona*, p. 27.
5. Adomnán, *Vitae Columbae*, bk. 3, ch. 4, in J. Marsden, *The Illustrated Columcille* (London, Macmillan, 1991), p. 155; see also pp. 28–30.
6. Information at the site, 2011.
7. B. Duffy, *Archaeology in County Sligo* (Sligo, Duchás, the Heritage Service, 1998), p. 28.
8. Information at the site, 2011.
9. Adomnán, *Vita Columbae*, bk. 2, ch. 26, in J. Marsden, *The Illustrated Columcille*, pp. 120.
10. Adomnán, *Vita Columbae*, bk. 3, ch. 22, in J. Marsden, *The Illustrated Columcille*, pp. 172–4.
11. Information at the site, 2011.
12. Kildare County Archaeology team, lecture at the site, June 2011.
13. M. Herity, *Gleanncholmcille*, (Dublin, Michael Herity, 1998), p. 5.
14. M. Herity, *Gleanncholmcille*, pp. 9, 60.
15. M. Herity, *Gleanncholmcille*, p. 35.
16. M. Herity, *Gleanncholmcille*, p. 16.
17. M. Herity, *Gleanncholmcille*, p. 34.

9. Three southern abbots

1. L. Barrow, *Glendalough and St Kevin* (Dundalk, Dundalgan Press, 1992), pp. 16–17.
2. C. Manning, *Early Irish Monasteries* (Dublin, Town House & Country House, 1995), pp. 30, 36.
3. Barrow, *Glendalough*, pp. 11–12.
4. Information at the site, 2011.
5. Information at the site, 2011.
6. Barrow, *Glendalough*, pp. 38–40.
7. Barrow, *Glendalough*, p. 24.
8. C. Manning, *Early Irish Monasteries*, pp. 22–3.
9. J.P. Hynes, *Kilmacduagh: a Short Guide* (Mold, J. P. Hynes, 1986), p. 8.

10. J.P. Hynes, *Kilmacduagh*, p. 9.
11. *Geinemain Molling ocus a bhetae*, ed. and transl. W. Stokes, as *The birth and life of St Mo Ling* (London, Harrison, 1907); *Corrigenda* in *Revue Celtique* vol. 28, 1907, pp. 70–72.
12. Information at the site, 2011.

10. Saints of Lough Erne

1. H. Hickey, *Images of Stone: Figure Sculpture of the Lough Erne Basin*, 2nd edition (Fermanagh, Fermanagh District Council, 1985), p. 69.
2. H. Hickey, *Images of Stone*, p. 69.
3. S. Mac Airt and G. Mac Niocaill, ed. and transl., *Annals of Ulster* (Dublin Institute for Advanced Studies, 1983).
4. Information at the site, 2011.
5. Information at the site, 2011.
6. I. Butler, 'A Journey to Lough Derg, *c.* 1749', ed. A. Cooper, *Journal of the Royal Society of Antiquaries of Ireland*, vol. 5, part 2, 1892, pp. 13–24.
7. R.A.S. Macalister, *Corpus Inscriptionum Insularum Celticum*, vol. 2 (Dublin, Stationery Office, 1949), p. 123.
8. H. Hickey, *Images of Stone*, p. 50.
9. H. Hickey, *Images of Stone*, p. 78.
10. W. Parke, *The Parish of Inishmacsaint* (Inishmacsaint, W. Parke, 1973), pp. 23–4.
11. W. Henry, *Upper Lough Erne in 1739* (Dublin, W. McGee, 1892).
12. H. Hickey, *Images of Stone*, pp. 23, 28, 112.
13. B. Duffy, *Archaeology in County Sligo* (Sligo, Duchás – the Heritage Service, 1998), p. 25.
14. F. Henry, *Irish Art during the Viking Invasions, 800–1020 AD* (Ithaca, New York, Cornell University Press, 1967), p. 192.
15. Information at the site, 2011.
16. Information at the site, 2011.
17. Information at the site, 2011.

11. Irish missionaries

1. J. Wooding, 'Monastic community in the Celtic West: Desert in the Ocean', lecture at Lampeter University, June 2008.
2. Eucherius, *In praise of the desert*, in T. and K. Vivian and J.B. Russell, *The Life of the Jura Fathers* (Kalamazoo, Michigan, Cistercian Publications, 1999).
3. J. Wooding, 'Irish and English Monks and Vikings: New reflections on the conversion of Scandinavia', lecture at Lampeter University, June 2005.
4. J. Wooding, 'Irish and English Monks and Vikings'.
5. J. Wooding 'Searching for the "desert" on land and sea', lecture at Lampeter University, June 2003.
6. Adomnán, *Vita Columbae*, bk. 1, ch. 6, in J. Marsden, *The Illustrated Columcille* (London, Macmillan, 1991), p. 64.
7. Adomnán, *Vita Columbae*, bk. 2, ch. 41, in J. Marsden, pp. 136–7.
8. Adomnán, *Vita Columbae*, bk. 1, ch. 20, in J. Marsden, pp. 70–72.
9. M. Priziac, *Bretagne des Saintes et des Croyances* (Grâces-Guingamp, Brittany, Ki-Dour Editions, 2002), pp. 200–201.

10. O. Davies, *Celtic Spirituality*, in *Classics of Western Spirituality* Series (New Jersey, Paulist Press, 1999), pp. 259–60.
11. G.S.M. Walker, (ed.), *Sancti Columbani Opera* (Dublin Institute for Advanced Studies, 1997), pp. 141–3.
12. O. Davies, *Celtic Spirituality*, p. 362.
13. N. Orme, *The Saints of Cornwall* (Oxford University Press, 2000), pp. 91–2.
14. R. Brunning and R. Croft, 'Somerset Archaeology 1998', Council for British Archaeology South West, no. 2, Winter/Spring 1999, p. 42.
15. Information at the site, 2011.
16. Information at the St Kilian's Heritage Centre, Mullagh, Cavan, 2011. This informative centre is open all summer, email: stkilianscentre@eircom.net.
17. It is now in the University Library, Würzburg, acquisition no. M.p.th.q.1a.
18. Information at the St Kilian's Heritage Centre, Mullagh, 2011.

12. Máelrúain and the Clients of God

1. M. Richter, *New Gill History of Ireland*, vol. 1, *Medieval Ireland: the Enduring Tradition* (Dublin, Gill and Macmillan, revised ed., 2005), p. 98.
2. M. Richter, *New Gill History of Ireland*, vol. 1, pp. 99–100.
3. K. Meyer, *Ancient Irish Poetry* (London, Constable, 1911), p. 86, with minor alterations; *Leabhar Breac*, p.106b.
4. G.F. Warner, *The Stowe Missal: MS D II 3 in the Library of the Royal Irish Academy, Dublin* (London, Henry Bradshaw Society, 1906), vol. 32.
5. V. Hull, (ed.), '*Apgitir Chrábaid*: the Alphabet of Piety', 38, Celtica, vol. 8, 1968, pp. 44–89.
6. *The Psalms: a new translation* (London, Collins, Fontana, 1967), with adjustments to reflect the Vulgate.
7. J. Borsje, 'Terrors in the night – war, love, death and demons', lecture at Lampeter University, June 2004.
8. W. Stokes and J. Strachan, *Thesaurus Palaeohibernicus* (Cambridge University Press, 1901–10), vol. 1, part 2.
9. J. Borsje, 'Terrors in the night – war, love, death and demons'.
10. E. Rees, *Christian symbols, ancient roots* (London, Jessica Kingsley, 1992), p. 94.
11. *Teagasg Máelrúain*, 4, quoted by M. Fraser, in 'The *Céli Dé* and the Authority of the Sacred', lecture at Lampeter University, June 2003.
12. M. Fraser, 'The *Céli Dé* and the Authority of the Sacred'.
13. O. Davies, *Celtic Christianity in Early Medieval Wales: the Origins of the Welsh Spiritual Tradition* (Cardiff University Press, 1996), pp. 45–8.
14. R. Van der Weyer, *Celtic Fire: an Anthology of Christian Literature* (London, Darton, Longman and Todd, 1990), pp. 70–72.
15. R. Van der Weyer, *Celtic Fire*, pp. 70–72.
16. O. Davies, *Celtic Christianity in Early Medieval Wales*, pp. 45–8.
17. J.S. Brewer, J.F. Dimock and G.F. Warner, eds., *Giraldus Cambrensis Opera*, Rolls Series 21, 8 vols (London, 1861–91), vol. 4, p. 167.
18. W. Follett, *Céli Dé in Ireland: Monastic Writing and Identity in the Early Middle Ages*, in *Studies in Celtic History* Series (Woodbridge, Suffolk, Boydell & Brewer, 2006), p. 3.
19. M. Chitty, *The Monks on Ynys Enlli*, Part 1, *c.* 500 AD – 1252 AD (Aberdaron, Mary Chitty, 1992), pp. 13–15.
20. M. Chitty, *The Monks on Ynys Enlli*, pp. 21–22.
21. W. Follett, *Céli Dé in Ireland*, p. 3.

22. S. Toulson, *Celtic Journeys in Scotland and the North of England* (London, Fount, 1995), p. 137.

23. R. Fawcett, *St Andrews Cathedral* (Edinburgh, Historic Scotland, 1993), p. 4.

24. R. Fawcett, *St Andrews Cathedral*, pp. 4–6.

25. O. Davies, *Celtic Christianity in Early Medieval Wales*, p. 47.

26. W. Follett, *Céli Dé in Ireland*, p. 3.

27. *Codex Insulensis*, Rawlinson B. 485, ff. 150–3.

28. *Vita*, 5, transl. D. Africa, 'The Life of the Holy Virgin Samthann' in *Medieval Hagiography: An Anthology*, ed. T. Head (New York, Garland, 2000), ch. 5, p. 104.

29. *Vita*, 25, transl. D. Africa, pp.108–9.

30. *Vita*, 23, transl. D. Africa, p.108.

31. *Vita*, 24, transl. D. Africa, p.108.

32. *Vita*, 6, transl. D. Africa, p.104.

33. *Vita*, 4, 9, 10, transl. D. Africa, pp. 103–5.

34. *Vita*, 7, 22, 12, transl. D. Africa, pp. 104, 108, 105.

35. Irenaeus of Lyons, *Adversus Haereses*, 4. 34. 5–7.

INDEX